Lucky Stars, Lucky Life

The Powerful Influence of Conjunctions in Astrology

By Alan Mayeda

Copyright Alan Mayeda, 2025

All Rights Reserved

Without limiting the rights reserved above under copyright, no part of this publication may be reproduced, stored in, or introduced into a retrieval system, or transmitted in any form or by any means (electronic, mechanical, photocopying, scanning, recording or otherwise), without written permission from both the author and the publisher, except in the case of brief quotations embodied in reviews and articles.
The scanning, uploading and distribution of this book via the Internet, or via any other means, without the written permission of the publisher is illegal and punishable by law. Please do not encourage electronic piracy of copyrighted materials.

ISBN: 978-0-86690-699-9

Requests and inquiries may be mailed to the publisher:

American Federation of Astrologers, Inc.
6553 S. Rural Road
Tempe, AZ 85283

www.astrologers.com

Lucky Stars, Lucky Life

ACKNOWLEDGEMENTS

I would like to extend my thanks to those who have encouraged me and individuals who remain nameless but mentioned in the book. I did not include their names as they are not well known to the general public.

I would like to thank the American Federation of Astrologers (AFA). The AFA, established in 1938 is one of the earliest American astrological organizations. In the early 1970s I attended the AFA annual conference held in Dallas, Texas. I wrote a brief article about the presentation given by the humanistic astrologer Dane Rudhyar.

Now that I am retired, I have been able to devote more time to my life-long interest, astrology.

I am indebted to AFA for publishing a few of my articles. I would like to thank Celeste Nash for her tireless work at the AFA and in particular Sheila Leedy at the AFA for working with this author to publish this book. The charts for this book were generated by Solar Fire Astrology. I would also like to thank the AstroData bank database and Astrotheme and their astrology database.

Table of Contents

Acknowledgements	iii
Preface	v
Introduction	vii
Chapter One	1
Chapter Two – Basics of Astrology	15
Chapter Three – Planetary Combinations	31
Chapter Four – The Cazimi	49
Chapter Five - Jupiter and Saturn	61
Chapter Six – The Moon's North Node	67
Chapter Seven – The Part of Fortune	79
Chapter Eight - Conclusion	85
Appendix I – Birth Data by Chapter	87
Appendix II – Lucky Stars - Planetary/ Special Conjunctions	89
Bibliography	139
Index	141
About the Author	143

PREFACE

When I began my study of astrology, I was taught to look at the major features, Sun, Moon and Ascendant and the "gestalt", or overall distribution of the planets around the zodiac. These were categorized into patterns espoused by Marc Edmund Jones. This topic has been covered in several books. This overall perspective was essential before proceeding into the weighing or the balance of signs, houses, etc. of the chart. We would look for planets that lie on critical degrees, the aspectual relationship between planets and closed aspect patterns in the chart.

The placement of the "high focus" planetary combinations, the conjunction, fascinated me. Planetary conjunctions are certainly not a new concept. Conjunctions are two or more planetary bodies, occupying approximately the same degree of longitude, and have been known as long as man observed the nighttime sky.

We have all heard the idiomatic term "Born Under a Lucky Star" and the phrase also appears in literature. It means to be born under fortunate circumstances in life and good luck in romance and life. I have often been asked what is the most successful sign of the zodiac? That depends on a few factors and the methodology used to determine success. I discovered that many of the successful individuals with two or more conjunctions seem to have the added quality for a greater success in life.

The two major aspects in any chart are the conjunction and opposition. Conjunctions are an important part of chart analysis, especially when aspected to other planets. We are unfortunately unable to observe the most important conjunction, that of the Sun and Moon. This is because this conjunction occurs during the day when the Moon and other planets are overcome by the brightness of the daytime Sun. This conjunction is only observed during a rare solar eclipse.

I have included conjunctions to the North Node and Part of Fortune as an additional factor to consider. The Moon's nodes identify its placement along the orbital path which intersects the plane of the Earth's orbit. It can have added significance especially for those born during a lunar or solar eclipse. I did not include major asteroids or major fixed stars as not everyone has a conjunction to these astrological points. Furthermore, pointing out a conjunction to a fixed star or major asteroid can be very selective and would require separate research.

There are a few conjunctions that offer the potential for great success and wealth. We commonly associate it with a planet conjunct to Jupiter. We are all familiar with Bill Gates, the founder of Microsoft, who has Jupiter conjunct Pluto. Throughout my research there is one conjunction pattern which I have uncovered, known as the cazimi of the Sun and Venus, indicative of great fame, success and wealth. It appears predominantly in the superior conjunction phase of the Sun and Venus.

As a student of astrology, when you run across more than one planetary conjunction, especially among young clients, it is worth noting their potential. Do they have talent in music or sports that might later show up in their career? You might want to see when this conjunction is stimulated by transit, secondary progression or other astrological forecasting techniques.

INTRODUCTION

Most everyone has wondered at one time or another if there is a secret to becoming rich and famous. Most people associate this with winning the lottery. Someone will eventually win the big lottery jackpot but the mathematical odds of winning are such that you have a better chance of being struck by lightning. That is precisely why the jackpot often grows ever larger only to attract the unsuspecting by fueling the frenzy.

Finding your "Lucky Stars" should not be confused with the keys to winning a lottery, a windfall or to foretell a fortunate event. Instead, "Lucky Stars" indicates someone who is likely talented, hardworking, with the promise of fame and great achievements. It shows someone blessed by providence with the rewards of achieving considerable fame and wealth.

Wealth is often a by-product of years of hard work, applying one's abilities and talents. This book will enable you to identify the extra boost given by your special qualities, opportunities through "Lucky Stars." They are more than just celestial lucky charms. Given the right combination of "Lucky Stars", a future of fame and fortune can be your birthright. As you go through this book you will see that there are a multitude of ways to become very famous and successful. Based on some difficult combination of planetary conjunctions, some may not have made the best or wisest choice of their freewill, leading to negative consequences.

It is claimed that ninety percent of Americans know their zodiacal sign and fewer know their Moon or Rising sign. The technique of "Lucky

Star, Lucky Life" has nothing to do with your Sun sign, fixed stars or numerology. What the general public has been exposed to are the general personality and temperament traits of stereotypical zodiacal signs to a particular Sun sign. This "pop", or popular astrology categorizes a person's personality type based on one of twelve Sun signs is simplistic but entertaining. In most cases it is simply what I consider pulp fiction. Unfortunately, this is what most people associate as astrology. I feel that it is not so much that few people take the time to explore this topic further but that most people prefer a life that is easily categorized and find comfort in the simplicities of life.

Astrology is not a religion or a belief system. It has survived the ridicule of scientists throughout the centuries. During the Renaissance, many of the great minds studied astrology. It was part of an academic discipline taught in western Europe up until the seventeenth century. Even after the geocentric model of Ptolemy was supplanted by the heliocentric model of Copernicus interest in astrology remains strong.

After exploring several different approaches to identify the keys to success, I have come up with the concept I call "Lucky Stars, Lucky Life." This book touches upon some of the basic concepts of astrology in very limited scope and breadth. Its purpose is to reveal the power of the planetary conjunctions and to identify astrological combinations or points that are likely to achieve a "Happy Life." This is not just another motivational self-help book. Unlike other books on success, this method is empirically based. The results of this research are simply amazing. Even the rich and famous are not aware of this concept of "Lucky Stars, Lucky Life" but have nonetheless have been fortunate as the recipients of its blessings.

I have often been asked "what is the most successful sign?" The answer is that there is no one zodiacal sign that ensures success. Each of the zodiacal signs have their strengths and weakness. A woman who owns over 30 rental properties told me that the most successful sign is her own Sun sign, Capricorn. To answer the question objectively one needs to define the criteria of success and a logical methodology. Often such studies are based on a limited sample size and taken at a certain point in time.

There have been some astrological studies conducted to find some relative correlation of certain professions (actors, journalists, artists, athletes etc.) to cosmic or astrological influences. This book provides a different approach to show that fame and success is not based on a person's Sun sign or some correlation or pattern to the cosmic roulette wheel. Each of us are unique individuals. What we consider uniqueness is in part based on planetary and special conjunctions which I refer to as "Lucky Stars."

A serious interest of astrology goes beyond knowing the qualities of a person's Sun, Moon or Rising sign. Astrology involves at least a basic understanding of signs, planets, houses, and planetary aspects. It involves studying mythology and the study of cycles. I do not generally accept the popular emphasis placed on a person's Sun or Moon sign since the Sun or Moon may not be well placed or integrated into the rest of the planets in the chart. The basis of the methodology of "Lucky Stars" has to do with planetary bodies that are closely aligned in an aspect known as a conjunction. On the other hand, the placement of your Sun or Moon when conjunct another planet, can be a "Lucky Star." It gives a unique quality to a person's character. We will also look at conjunctions to the Moon's North Node, and the Part of Fortune as well as planets to the four key points in the natal chart: Ascendant, Medium Coeli (MC), Descendant and Imum Coeli (IC).

This book will show you how to find your "Lucky Stars" and associated meanings. You may even have more than one Lucky Star. Although well known to astrologers, the conjunction aspect has never been presented as a "Lucky Star." Most people may have a planetary and/or a special conjunction and are not aware of it. When the potential of the "Lucky Star" is realized it can propel your destiny into a more rewarding life than you may have thought possible.

This book will not tell you when you will achieve happiness and good fortune. Like life itself, it involves a continuous process of growth, experiences and a state of mind. In astrology this is manifested in cycles. Enjoy what you do in furtherance of the good of society and should you be recognized for your efforts you will be rewarded. That is why well know celebrities in the entertainment field, famous sports figures, and business figures are revered and well rewarded.

Serious astrologers may criticize this book for its simplistic approach. By the way I have tried to apply the most basic aspect, the conjunction, in a chart. It is my hope this book might expand the reader's consciousness and curiosity to further explore this ancient art. The approach in this book in no way can replace an in-depth chart analysis or forecasting by a competent astrologer.

Some see life as a series of lucky breaks. This requires that you possess some talent or skill to begin with. Some are fortunate to be born with an innate talent in life. It's good to know your limitations and your assets and to take full advantage of the qualities of your "Lucky Star." Some may take a while to realize and develop the qualities that they were born with. Even having just a single "Lucky Star" can lead to an amazing and rewarding life.

This book will explore a few different planetary conjunctions that are more promising than others. Among the most auspicious "Lucky Stars" is the cazimi of the Sun and Venus. An entire chapter is devoted to this unique planetary conjunction.

Using this book, you will learn the technique to find the "Lucky Stars" for yourself and your loved ones. I have divided the conjunctions into two categories. The first, or Category I conjunctions, are simply planetary conjunctions. For this category all you need to know is your date, month and year of birth. I've included in this category the Moon's North Node. Category II conjunctions are what I refer to as special conjunctions. These special conjunctions can add an additional impetus towards your good fortune and karmic destiny. In other words, the combination of the Category I and Category II conjunctions serve as an invisible link between man's material or mundane affairs and the evolution of the soul.

We are more than just our physical body. We are all energy and spiritual beings. As small as we are, our energies are connected to the energies of the cosmos. In metaphysics this is referred to as the microcosm and the macrocosm. Astrology is just a tool that can demonstrate this connection. So, let's get started to see what secrets astrology has to offers with respect to your "Lucky Star(s) and possibly a "Lucky Life."

CHAPTER ONE

Have you ever wondered why some people are able to attain fame and fortune while others are not? This book offers a unique perspective to help you understand how "Lucky Stars" work and help you understand your relationship to others and your destiny. The "Lucky Star(s) offer the "seed potential," as natural gifts or qualities when fully actualized that can lead to a life of fame, honors and in the end considerable wealth.

The beauty of "Lucky Stars, Lucky Life" is based on its simplicity. It is not based on your zodiacal Sun sign, constellations, fixed stars or numerology. It does involve some of the most basic concepts of astrology. What we are looking for is a specific astrological aspect known as a conjunction in your chart.

Identifying your "Lucky Star(s)" requires little or no knowledge of astrology. The next chapter provides a basic introduction or review of mundane astrology. It uses the symbolic language, or terminology of western or tropical astrology. Throughout the ages man has tried to understand the meaning of life with respect to the universe through symbolic or metaphysical means. Initially, this gave rise to the meanings associated with the constellations of the zodiac, the meaning and naming of planets due to myths and legends of ancient gods. As the ancient Greeks looked up at the night sky they observed two kinds of celestial objects; fixed stars and what they referred to as wandering stars. Today we know the wandering stars as the five visible planets: Mercury, Venus, Mars, Jupiter, and Saturn.

The concept of "Lucky Stars" includes all the wandering planets including the modern planets, Uranus, Neptune and Pluto.

It also makes use of the North Node and Part of Fortune. Just to let you know, there is a branch of traditional astrology known as Hellenistic astrology that does not use the modern planets in their interpretation.

I have divided "Lucky Stars" into two categories. To find the Category I "Lucky Stars" you simply need to know your date of birth, month and year you were born. You can easily find Category I conjunctions by using your cell phone and by typing in your year of birth and ephemeris. Then go to Astro.com or Café Astrology and scroll down to find your month and date of birth. You can then see if you have any planets in the same sign that are conjunct with each other. The Category I "Lucky Stars" mainly affect your unique temperament and character based on the interaction of the planet energies. If you were born when the Sun was conjunct a planet it would add a special boost or zest to your individuality. These planetary combinations, known as conjunctions, are like adding spice in the recipe of life. Most people are likely to have a "Lucky Star." I will show that it may only take a single special conjunction to achieve a "Lucky Life." Even if you do not have a "Lucky Star" I will direct you to a few secondary features to look for in your chart

To find the Category II Special Conjunctions you will need to know your time and place of birth. This information is needed to determine your Ascendant, Part of Fortune and the house divisions. Thanks to the wonders of modern technology anyone knowing their time of birth and place of birth can easily get their chart done. All it takes is a device with internet access. If you don't have an internet device, just go to any library. Simply input the necessary information to generate a free natal chart. I suggest you print a hard copy, preferably in color, of your birth chart for future reference.

If you don't know your time of birth, the computer might set your time of birth at a default setting of noon, the midpoint of the day. Even if you think you know the approximate time of birth you should disregard any conjunctions to the Ascendant, or the other three major points of the chart. The reason for the importance of the time of birth is that the Ascendant moves one degree every four minutes. A person's Ascendant or Rising Sign would change every two hours. If you experiment with different birth times you will notice a change in the Rising Sign/Ascendant, and the axis points. The relationship between the planets will remain mostly the same but their hemispheric orientation will change. So, if you don't know your time and place of birth, the Category II special planetary conjunctions will be questionable.

The non-planetary Category II special conjunctions identify the forces outside of our control, much like fate, preordained to fulfill one's destiny. The special conjunctions use the non-physical or mathematical points known as the Part of Fortune and the Moon's North Node. These points are separately covered in later chapters. When you actualize your "Lucky Stars," you are likely to attain the prospects of a "Lucky Life". By "Lucky Life" I am referring to a deep purposeful meaning to your life and rewards of considerable wealth. Think of your life accomplishments as part of your rich legacy in fulfillment of your destiny.

Conjunctions are easier to see when a person looks at a natal chart. Two planets that are conjunct each other are usually positioned in the same sign. In some cases, you might find one of the two planets that are conjunct on the cusp of a sign. This happens when one of the two planets is situated near the end of one sign and the other at the beginning of the next sign. A planet at the end of one sign will tend to absorb the qualities of the sign it is about to enter.

I have often been asked "How many secret or "Lucky Stars" are there?" There are about a hundred. There are forty-five Category I planetary combinations or conjunctions. Then there are conjunctions of the planets to the Moon's North Node. The Moon's North Node will be covered further in a separate chapter. Additionally, there are conjunctions of the planets to the Part of Fortune. Finally, there may be conjunctions of the Sun, Moon, planets, North Node, and the Part of Fortune to the four major points of the chart that need to be considered.

The conjunction is the most basic and strongest aspect in the natal chart. The conjunction aspect as expressed by astrologer, Marc Edmund Jones, indicates it as an emphasis of effort in direct purpose or immediate concern. He considers the awareness or directed effort as if the conjunction were to appear in the first sign of the zodiac, Aries.

The three main features most people are familiar with in Western astrology are the Sun, Moon and Ascendant. When the Sun and Moon, Ascendant and the Sun, or Moon and the Ascendant are in the same sign, for example Cancer, they are referred to as a double Cancer. In a rare case if you have all three (Sun, Moon and Ascendant) in the same sign, such as Virgo, you could describe yourself as a rare triple Virgo. The statistical odds of being born as a double sign is one in one hundred and forty-four and those having all three major features in the same sign is one in seventeen hundred and twenty-eight. (Twelve times twelve times twelve).

One such example is the natal chart of Katy Perry, American singer, songwriter and TV personality. You will see in her chart the Big Three (Ascendant, Sun and Moon) are all in the same sign making her a triple Scorpio. In addition to having the three major features in Scorpio she has Mercury, Saturn and Pluto in Scorpio. There is an obvious lack of air qualities in her chart. In other words, there are no planets in the air signs of Gemini, Libra or Aquarius. With an overwhelming emphasis in the water sign of Scorpio there is a tendency to relate more instinctually from her feelings, intuition and emotions rather than intellectually or rationally.

This is partially offset with Mercury conjunct her Ascendant giving her good communication skills. With a sharp mind, she has no difficulty expressing herself and her opinions. A person with this combination might consider expressing their creative energy by writing, screen writing, teaching, lecturing, acting, or even conducting a solo performance.

All the planets located in each hemisphere of the chart indicate a particular life focus. All her planets are in the left half or eastern hemisphere of the chart, and according to Marc Edmund Jones, this is characteristic of a tight bundle pattern. If we ignore the aspects to the Midheaven (MC), her planets are all within three signs and which indicates an intense focus of energies in a very narrow area of life experiences. Her planets are more focused than most, as her planets fit in a typical bundle pattern where all her planets are within four signs or 120 degrees.

The powerful Sun partile Pluto is significant as it serves as the leading planet in the bundle pattern. She may live a self-contained and a life of narrow focus which is characteristic of a bundle pattern. The positive feature is that it helps to focus and concentrate upon her creative skills and abilities. This narrow focus may come with a feeling of isolation being in her twelfth house. It may also be transformative holding the keys to the unconscious and spiritual transformation. Loyalty, duty, and responsibility are no stranger to a person with Moon conjunct Saturn in the first house.

Say we did not know the time of her birth and simply use the "Lucky Star" method. We still can reveal a lot about her. Looking at an ephemeris, we can easily notice the strong water emphasis with both her Sun and Moon as well as three planets (Mercury, Saturn and Pluto) in the sign of Scorpio. We can also notice the tight distribution of planets in just the three signs of Scorpio, Sagittarius and Capricorn. She has two Category I planetary conjunctions both involving the primary lights,

Sun and Moon, conjunct two powerful planets in the sign of Scorpio. She has two partile conjunctions. Her Sun is in a partile aspect to Pluto and her Moon is also in a partile conjunction to Saturn. Both Pluto and Saturn are often considered uneasy and challenging planets. They involve sacrifices of time and commitment. The partile aspect of Sun and Pluto serves as an incubator leading to transformation into the mystery and spiritual domain of the twelfth house. With such strong planetary conjunctions and concentration of planets in Scorpio, a water sign indicates a person who is passionate with deep and intense feelings. Pluto is the modern ruler of Scorpio, indicating a strong sense of power, control and ambition. Having such a strong Scorpio emphasis, the positive and negative qualities characteristics of Scorpio would apply to her. The Moon in a partile aspect to Saturn may have influenced her family dynamics in her early years.

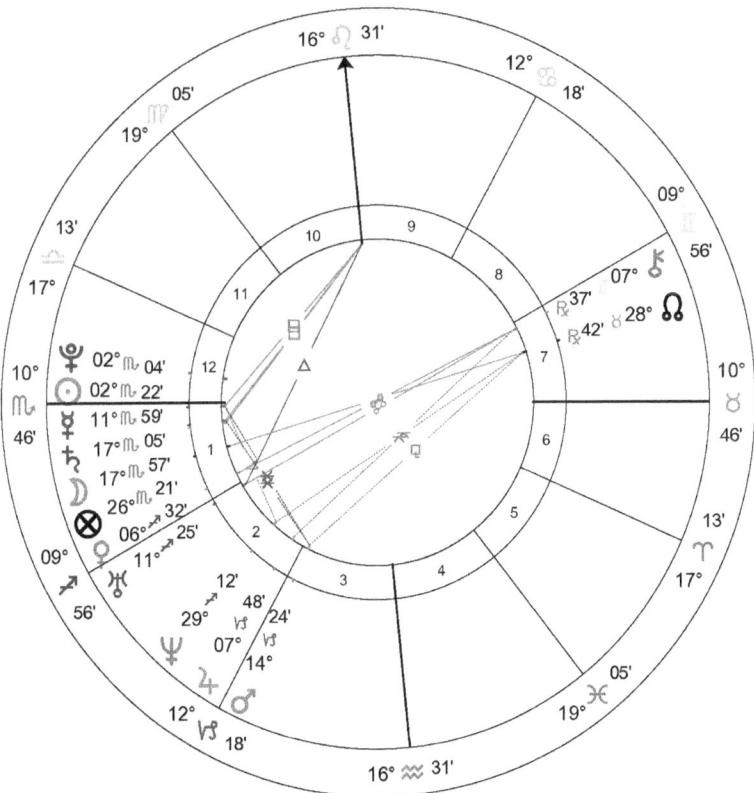

Natal Chart for Katy Perry, 10/25/1984 07, 07:58 AM, Santa Barbara, California

In contrast to a person who has a strong focus upon a single zodiacal sign, as in the case of Katy Perry, I have heard some people tell me that they do not relate to their Sun sign. This is not unusual but understandable once the natal chart is constructed. The Sun may not be well integrated or aspected to other planets in the chart. Having a "Lucky Star" or a conjunction avoids this problem by not of strictly relying upon a person's Sun sign but by its direct relationship to another planet.

The system of "Lucky Stars" lies in its simplicity. It does not attempt to distinguish the interpretation of two planetary bodies that may be moving towards each other (applying) or moving away (separating) from each other or if it is retrograde. It does not matter if a planet is travelling faster or slower than its average speed. This may occur when a planet is about to go stationary before it goes retrograde or when it is about to transition from retrograde to direct.

What is a retrograde planet? It describes the apparent motion of a planet as it appears to being going backwards relative to the Earth's perspective. We all know that planets do not actually go backwards. Imagine runners running in a circular track where one runner in the middle lane overtakes another runner giving the illusion that the other runner is going backward or retrograde. You might think of the runners in the inner lane as planets within the earth's orbit and those in the outside lanes as outer planets. The psychological and mundane interpretations of retrograde planets are covered in numerous astrological books.

Other than the Sun and Moon, all planets go retrograde sometime throughout the year. Mercury, the closest planet to the Sun, goes retrograde more frequently but for shorter periods than the outer planets. The retrograde period ranges from twenty-four days for Mercury, forty-two days for Venus and eighty days for Mars. The planets further from the earth can go retrograde for months. A retrograde planet is represented by a Rx after the planet in the ephemeris and in the chart. It is likely that you may have one or more retrograde planets.

The conjunction of two planets is easy to spot. Planets that are in conjunction ideally occupy the same degree in terms of longitude and are usually in the same sign. There are no hard and fast rules as the orbs of influence are given as guidelines. I have used an orb of three degrees between planets, and the Moon's North Node and the Part of Fortune. I set an orb of five degrees when it involves the Sun and Moon to other planets.

Typically, the orbs for the Sun or Moon when used in the interpretation of a natal chart may use slightly wider orbs. By extending the orbs by even a couple of degrees would increase the list of names in Appendix II considerably. Conjunctions that are just outside the limits I have set are identified by a bracket around the conjunction.

Two planetary bodies that are tighter or closer to each other naturally have a stronger influence than one that is further apart. The term partile aspect is used to denote a conjunction that is less than one degree of each other. Partiles are simply identified as (P). You are more likely to relate or feel the nature of the planets that are in a partile conjunction due to their compelling influence. Whenever there are two planets that are tightly aligned to each other, you might want to check if they are aspected or influenced by another planet especially by an opposition aspect.

The earlier in life you develop your talents or skills the better. Knowing that you have a particular interest, or talent will enable you to focus your energies to nurture those talents perhaps into a successful lifetime adventure. It can take some time to shift one's focus when you may be busy just working to survive. Others may be busy investing in a career that simply provides a comfortable living. A comfortable career may not spark their passion to achieve their true potential. There are countless cases when a young adult went to college to pursue a career based on expectations of their parents, only to find at some point in their life, they decide to follow their own interest or passion. Some need an inner motivation or opportunity to unleash their creative energies. Some call it finding your passion. Age is no barrier to exploring new outlets to achieve your own goals and potential.

One such example is Ann Mary Robertson Moses, affectionately known as Grandma Moses. She was born September 7, 1860, (time unknown) in Greenwich, NY. On the date of her birth there were two Category I planetary conjunctions: Mercury conjunct Saturn and Moon conjunct Uranus. These conjunctions facilitate mental focus, concentration, creativity and originality. At the age of seventy-eight she took up painting and continued to paint until she passed away at age ninety-one. She became a renown American folk artist and had her works exhibited internationally. Her paintings sold for over a million dollars.

If you ever had your birth chart cast, you will know that your Sun, Moon and planets are plotted against a background of the twelve zodiacal signs and houses. The horoscope is divided horizontally along the East-West as well as vertically along its North-South axis, forming the four quadrants of the chart. The horizon defines the separation between what is visible (day) and the invisible (night), or what is seen and what is not. On the eastern horizon is your Ascendant and on the opposite end, the western horizon, is the Descendant. Then there is the MC and IC axis which divides the chart between the eastern and western hemisphere.

The Sun rises on the most eastern point, the Ascendant. The Ascendant represents sunrise, thus the term Rising sign. The upper most meridian point is known as the Midheaven or Medium Coeli (MC). The Medium Coeli means "middle of the heavens" and is the highest point in your chart. It marks the cusp of the tenth house and the height of your public persona. In other words, your social standing, achievements, accomplishments, and reputation. At the other end of the axis, is the Imum Coeli IC), the "lowest part of the heavens" or sometimes referred to as "Little Midheaven". Any planet situated on the Ascendant, MC, Descendant or IC) is important. Then the Sun continues its journey to dawn, represented by the Descendant, and IC and finally crossing the Ascendant only to repeat its cycle all over again.

In a natal chart, the planets are situated in a background of zodiacal signs and houses. What are houses in astrology? Houses are areas in which life is experienced. Unlike signs of the zodiac, the twelve houses are arranged clockwise in the natal chart, the astrological houses are arranged in a counterclockwise direction starting from the Ascendant.

The astrological houses are durational in nature. In other words, Category II special conjunctions are based on the fourth dimensional level as they are based on time and location. Category II conjuncts depend on the house divisions of the chart and the division of the major axis points of the chart. Human experience and values are expressed in terms of consciousness and power that operate in the various houses.

Unlike zodiacal signs which are divided into equal increments of thirty degrees, houses divisions may not be equally divided. It mainly depends on the latitude you were born. Charts in this book use the Placidus house system.

Each of the houses is associated with certain compartments or areas of life expression. We will focus on the cusps of the first, fourth, seventh, and tenth houses coinciding with the four major points in the chart. The cusp of the first house is known as the Ascendant. It has the characteristics of the first sign of the zodiac, Aries, ruled by Mars, the center of the field of one's individual personality.

In traditional astrology the first house has to do with one's individual self-expression and appearance.

The quadrant beginning with the fourth house is the IC. Like the fourth zodiacal sign, Cancer, it represents an individual's sense of home and feeling of security. At the seventh house cusp, the Descendant, having developed his/her talents through the cooperative and harmonious effort with others. The tenth house represents one's achievements, recognition and honors by the public. Consequently, conjunctions in the tenth house or near the MC are symbolic of culmination in one's career.

The interpretation of conjunctions in the various houses will depend only if we have an accurate chart. Without an accurate time of birth or birth chart, any conjunction would rely more in the zodiacal sign in which the conjunction is situated, as the major house divisions are unknown.

Here is a summary of the traditional terms what each of the houses represent.

First House: It is the house of the Self. It defines the personality as distinguished from individuality (Sun). Planets in this house give an understanding of who you are and how others perceive you in terms of physical appearance, personal disposition, and outlook. It is a sign of one's self-centered awareness.

Second House: Like the second sign of the zodiac, Taurus, it represents material possessions and personal sense of security, and the concept of value and worth.

Third House: Like the third sign of the zodiac, Gemini, it is about communication. It closely relates to one's immediate environment, siblings and short journeys, and all manners of communication. Those with a third house emphasis are linked to mental processes, thinking and writing. Those with a third house emphasis find careers involved in writing, broadcasting, advertising, social media, as well working with small children and animals.

Fourth House: At the cusp of the fourth house is the Lower Midheaven. Like the zodiacal sign Cancer, it is about the comfort security of home and family. It describes your home life, roots and family relations, and psychological foundations. It sets the framework for spiritual happiness and joy in life. As such, planets conjunct the cusp of the fourth house, or the IC, can have a very powerful influence.

Fifth House: This house is related to creativity, self-expression, children, recreation, entertainment, speculation, and leisure activities.

Sixth House: This house is related to service, daily routine, working environment, health, and employer-employee relationships.

Seventh House: The cusp of the seventh house is referred to as the Descendant. This house represents one's personal identity through relationships or partnership with others. It is in contrast or opposition of the Aries quality of discovery, self-awareness and energy of "I am." In the seventh house the individual faces social interaction represented by Libra. It is the house of partnerships, both personal (marriage) as well as business relationships.

Eighth House: In contrast to individual possessions and wealth of the second house, the eighth house has to do with wealth but in terms of other people's money or shared resources such as inheritances and trusts. The eighth house also deals with sex, death, rebirth and regeneration. It is also the house of mysteries with close ties to the hidden knowledge of the occult and paranormal activities that cannot be explained by logic and science.

Ninth House: This is the house of higher learning, such as philosophy, law, travel, religion, often involving foreign culture and overseas travel.

Tenth House: The cusp of the tenth house is the MC. It is the house of one's profession, personal honor, achievements, and social status.

Eleventh House: This is the house of friendships and groups. It is also about your hopes, wishes, and desires. Identification with broader social or group objectives.

Twelfth House: The last house is sometimes associated with endings and the later stage in life. Here some individuals end up living alone in a nursing home, retirement facility or assisted care facility.

It is the house of institutions, secrets, escapism, and confinement. Associated with the twelfth house are hospitals, living in a cloistered environment as well as confinement in an institution or prison.

It is also associated with the house for martyrs. It is the house of seclusion and solitude where one can recover from physical and mental issues, meditate, and take the time to recharge one's batteries.

In the book "*The Count of Monte Cristo*," the protagonist, Edmond Dantes, as a young man is falsely arrested and imprisoned without trial. Over his long imprisonment in a grim island fortress, an older fellow prisoner befriends him by educating him and tells him about a secret hidden treasure. The twelfth house reminds me of his period of confinement and the knowledge he receives during his confinement.

Following the death of his friend, Dantes manages to escape, recovers the secret treasure and seeks retribution from those who wronged him.

The twelfth house is also about your storehouse of hidden strengths and weaknesses. Like the sign of Pisces, you may be very sensitive and introspective, and a willingness to surrender or sacrifice oneself. It also represents collective unconsciousness and selfless service to humanity.

A conjunction can appear as a paired combination of two planets simply conjunct with each other or within a cluster of planets. When three or more planets are clustered close together it is referred to as a stellium. A stellium adds a stronger influence than just a conjunction adding considerable nuance to an individual's character. A stellium can fall into two categories. In an ideal stellium, the grouping of planets in a conjunction to one another can be found in the same sign or house.

The other category is what I refer to as a "stretch stellium" where the planets may be separated by as much as 8 – 10 degrees. The planets within a stretch stellium may or may not fall in the same sign or house. Also, one of the end planets may be aspected to another planet in the chart but may not be aspected to the planet in the other end of the stellium. In a stretch stellium the energies can be diffused making interpretation a little more complicated. If you run across a "stretch stellium" I suggest you look to see if there is a dominant planet by rulership or look for a partile conjunction within the stellium. For additional information about stelliums and planetary patterns I refer you to the book "*Discover the Aspect Pattern in Your Birth Chart*" by Glenn Mitchell.

When looking at a natal chart you can easily notice any conjunctions, the North Node, the Part of Fortune as well as the lines of aspectual relationships between the planets. The chart also displays the house divisions. It is so much more convenient than simply relying on an electronic or physical ephemeris. Depending on the website or astrological program used it may or may not show the Part of Fortune. Instructions to calculate it manually are given in Chapter 7, Part of Fortune.

The next chart is that of Rhonda Byrne. She was born on March 12, 1951, in Melbourne, Australia (time unknown). Prior to becoming rich and famous, she lived a comfortable life with a career as a television writer and producer. Her life changed dramatically with the publication of her book "*The Secret*". The DVD and sales of the book grossed over $300 million. That book sold over 30 million copies and was translated into 40 languages.

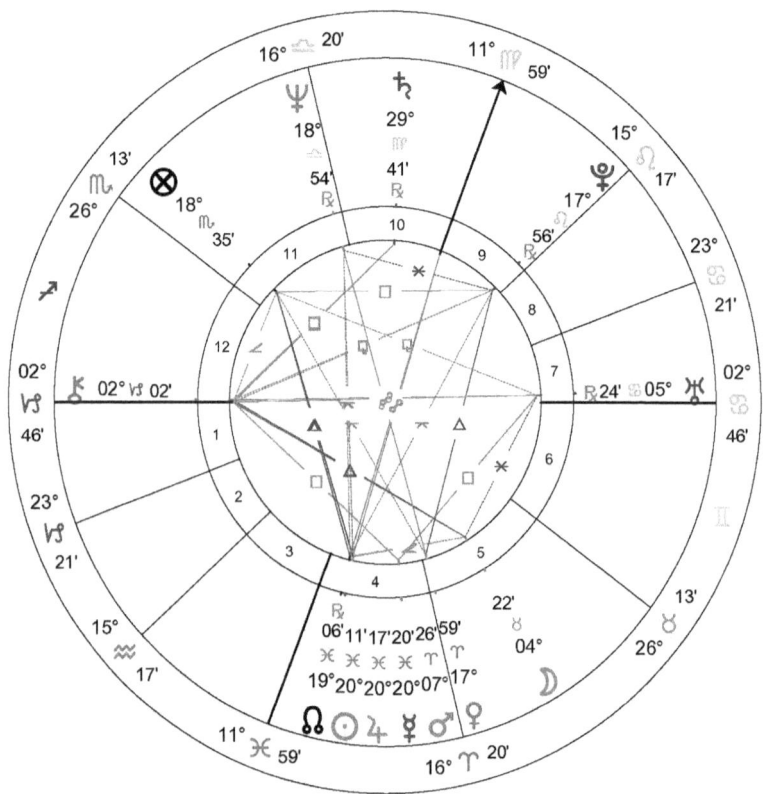

Natal Chart for Rhonda Byrne, 03/21/1951, Melbourne, Australia

Looking at her chart, she has a stellium of three planets and the North Node all within three degrees in the sign of Pisces. Within the stellium are two planetary partile conjunctions: Sun and Mercury and Sun and Jupiter. Mercury is the planet that has to do with communication, writing and the dissemination of ideas.

Her Sun (20 Pisces 41) and Jupiter (20 Pisces 45) are separated by just 16 minutes. The stellium serves not only to bring about positive energy on a personal level but imparts the laws of metaphysics that thoughts create reality and the attraction of positive thoughts of abundance. You might also note there is a tight partile opposition aspect between Venus (18 Aries 32) and Neptune (18 Libra 54). The planet Venus has to do with wealth and Neptune, the planet of spirituality and the power of one's creative subconscious.

Another example of having a propitious combination of the Sun, Jupiter and North Node, all within one degree of each other, can be found in the chart of Barbara Stanwyck, actress of film, stage, and screen.

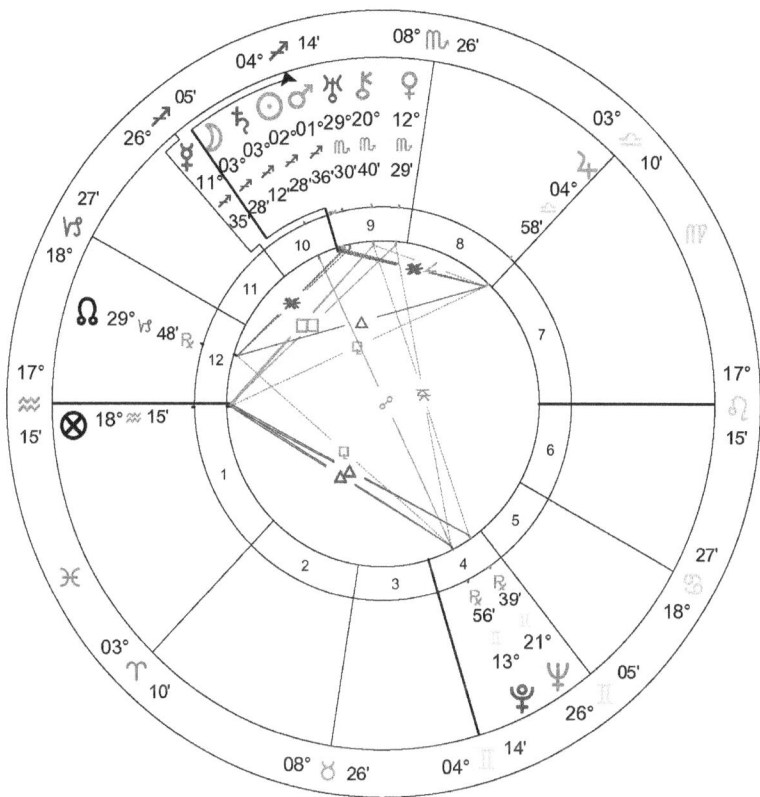

Natal Chart for Lucky Luciano, 11/24/1897, 12:00 PM, Lercara Friddi, Italy

Another example of the tremendous power of the conjunctions within a stellium can be found in the next natal chart of Lucky Luciano, the godfather of organized crime. This Sicilian born, American mobster, was the head of American organized crime in the 1930's. Like many gangsters and cult leaders he used fear, cohesion, and intimidation to achieve his ends. If all else failed, he would resort to violence. He was the first boss of what was to be known as the Genovese crime family.

Lucky Stars, Lucky Life 13

His Sun, Moon, Mars, Saturn and Uranus are within four degrees of each other in Sagittarius. This stellium in Sagittarius indicates a person with a high degree of mission and purpose. This is a person that is confident, egocentric and arrogant. As a double Sagittarius he has especially strong Sagittarius qualities to achieve his goals through management of his will and power. With Mars and Uranus as part of this stellium indicates he would impose his will on others. It also indicates a person who can be temperamental, forceful and domineering.

His chart is an example of the Sun and Moon not only in the same sign but conjunct each other which takes on the qualities of the New Moon. Additionally, the placement of the sign and house of the Sun and Moon takes on greater importance upon an individual's identity and sense of self. One book that covers the placement of the Sun and Moon by house is *"Behind the Horoscope"* by Wendell C. Perry. Another added feature to consider is whenever the Sun and Moon are in a tight conjunction, their Part of Fortune will lie on the Ascendant. Lucky's ambition and drive enabled him to rise in power and fame as the planets in his stellium were all auspiciously conjunct his MC, the house of fame and success.

CHAPTER TWO

BASICS OF ASTROLOGY

Astrology is not a religion or belief system. It has no set of philosophical doctrines, organization or hierarchical structure characteristic of organized religions or belief of some divine being. The noted astrologer, Dane Rudhyar, explained astrology as the study of correlations that can be established between the positions of celestial bodies around the Earth and physical events or psychological and social changes in the consciousness of man. To understand this correlation involves an understanding of the language of astrology. Its most fundamental components include the zodiacal signs, planets, houses and aspects.

The Earth travels, as it tilts on its axis, on its annual trek around the Sun. This journey is against the backdrop of what we know as months and each of the signs of the zodiac. I will not go into the archetypical meanings associated with each of the zodiacal signs as you know doubt are familiar with them as they are popularized in books and magazines. The general public is often exposed to a particular author's interpretation of both the positive/negative personality traits.

Getting back to the basics. Each sign of the zodiac is either a masculine or feminine sign, by element (fire, earth, air and water) and one of three modes (cardinal, fixed or mutable).

The gender and modality will not apply in the concept of "Lucky Stars." Each of the twelve signs of the zodiac operates in one of four elements (fire, earth, air, or water) and in one of three modes (cardinal, fixed or mutable) making up the twelve signs of the zodiac.

Sign	Masc/Fem	Ruler	Modality	Element	Characteristics/Traits
Aries	Masculine	Mars	Cardinal	Fire	Independent, bold, competitive, enthusiastic, impulsive
Taurus	Feminine	Venus	Fixed	Earth	Stable, practical, stubborn, responsible
Gemini	Masculine	Mercury	Mutable	Air	Communicative, inquisitive, curious
Cancer	Feminine	Moon	Cardinal	Water	Nurturing, intuitive, loyal
Leo	Masculine	Sun	Fixed	Fire	Self-expressive, confident, creative, seeks attention, pride, desire for power
Virgo	Feminine	Mercury	Mutable	Earth	Perfectionist, practical, analytical, critical
Libra	Masculine	Venus	Cardinal	Air	Diplomatic, cooperative, fair minded, social, artistic sense
Scorpio	Feminine	Pluto/Mars	Fixed	Water	Intense but secretive, powerful, resourceful
Sagittarius	Masculine	Jupiter	Mutable	Fire	Expansive, generous, likes travel and outdoors
Capricorn	Feminine	Saturn	Cardinal	Earth	Hard working, goal oriented, good managers, ambitious
Aquarius	Masculine	Uranus/Saturn	Fixed	Air	Reformer, original, independent, humanitarian
Pisces	Feminine	Neptune/Jupiter	Mutable	Water	Highly intuitive, sensitive, gentle, can be the victim or martyr

	Cardinal	Fixed	Mutable
Fire	Aries	Leo	Sagittarius
Earth	Capricorn	Taurus	Virgo
Air	Libra	Aquarius	Gemini
Water	Cancer	Scorpio	Pisces

What is an aspect in astrology? It is the angular relationship of two bodies relative to each other. It helps further to understand the relationship of the planets within the signs and houses in the natal chart. In the language of astrology one can think of aspects like the verb, in the parts of speech, which explain the relationship between planets. One must understand those aspects within the context of the cyclic nature of planetary bodies.

The angular relationship between planets is referred to as aspects. There are four major aspects based on the division of the 360-degree circle by one, two, three, and four. They are referred to as the conjunction (0 degrees), opposition (180 degrees), trine (120 degrees) and square (90 degrees). Then there are minor aspects that are based on further divisions of the circle.

It is not the distance of the planetary bodies from the Earth that provides its significance to astrologers but their longitude and angular relationship to one another and to key points in the natal chart. The planets all revolve around the Sun in cycles. Our lives occur within a giant cosmic timepiece involving smaller cycles within larger cycles.

The basis of "Lucky Stars" is planetary combinations, specifically the conjunction aspect. Once you find the conjunction(s) in your chart or ephemeris, you can use Appendix II in this book to find certain qualities that you share in common with other noted personalities. Many are well known in their field for having achieved their success through their talents and creative skills.

The outer planets (Uranus, Neptune and Pluto) take longer to revolve around the Sun and often are viewed as generational planets. For example, Saturn and Uranus conjoin each other every forty-five years, thirty-five to thirty-seven years for Saturn and Neptune and roughly five hundred years for Neptune and Pluto. They are interpreted in terms of deep subconscious or on a deeper psychological level or in terms of broader geo-political changes. The trans-Saturnian planets, Uranus, Neptune and Pluto are said to affect an individual on the subconscious level.

Saturn represents tradition, institutions, and authority figures. In politics when Saturn reacts with Neptune it is like acid wearing away the structure of established institutions. From a geopolitical perspective the winds of political change started with the Saturn conjunct Uranus in October 1988, followed by Saturn conjunct Neptune. An example of the generational impact is the conjunction of Saturn and Neptune which occurs roughly every thirty-five to thirty-seven years.

The last conjunction was in the sign of Capricorn which occurred in February 1989, in June 1989 when both planets were retrograde, and then in November 1989. This conjunction symbolizes the dissolution of the foundations of society by eroding existing boundaries. We saw the fall of the Berlin Wall (November 1989), the riots in Tiananmen Square in China (April – June 1989) and the eventual collapse of the Soviet empire.

The outer planets, moving much slower than the inner planets, are likely to be conjunct each other for a couple of weeks. As they form a conjunction the two planets may be in the same sign for several months. The next Saturn/Neptune conjunction is set to occur when both planets enter the critical 0 degrees Aries in April/May 2025 during the second Trump administration. Both planets will remain in Aries until Saturn enters Taurus in 2028.

When Saturn and other trans Saturnian planets enter the cardinal signs of Aries, Cancer, Libra or Capricorn they can be seen as precursors of major social change. This can be seen in the US chart as these generational planets have affected major periods in US history. How significant is the influence of Uranus? Uranus has a cycle of eighty-four years. The cycle of Uranus in the US chart has been coincident with periods of turmoil and war. The second Uranus return occurred in June 1860 during the American Civil War. The third Uranus return occurred the end of May 1944 (D-Day was June 6) during WWII. The next Uranus return will be in May 2028.

During the US presidential election Donald Trump made many bold campaign promises. We can expect dramatic changes domestically and a shift on international relations. Will the trend towards isolationism and a change in international relations result in a wavering of our support to our allies? Our support to Ukraine and Taiwan remains uncertain. Will we see a demise of Putin and the Russian Federation? We can expect political and economic turmoil, but we should not rule out the possibly of a sudden occurrence of a natural or man-made traumatic event. One should not rule out a major constitutional crisis or unforeseen international military conflict.

As a conjunction between the outer planets is quite rare, we should not ignore the meaning between the personal planets to the outer planets. To understand the uniqueness of the blended meaning of a planetary combination we first must understand the astrological meanings associated with each of the planets.

For the sake of convenience, astrologers refer to the Sun and Moon as planets. So as not to overwhelm the reader I will provide just a condensed view of the meanings of the planets.

SUN

Our Sun happens to be one of billions of stars in our Milky Way galaxy. The distance from the Earth to our star is roughly ninety-four million miles. It is the center or nucleus of our solar system . It is the heart of our solar system and the star which our family of planets revolve. Through its heat, light and energy it sustains life on our planet.

The Sun is a key component of the natal chart acting together with the Moon and Ascendant. The symbol of the Sun represents our creative self and is vital to our individual integration, and self-expression. Any planet conjunct the Sun is important as it demonstrates how our ego relates to the outer world. It represents our personality and development of our drive and self-worth.

MOON

The Moon is the only satellite of Earth. It also reflects vital light and energy from the Sun. It has the fastest cycle being that it revolves around the Earth. The Moon is the closest astronomical body to the Earth. Its distance is roughly 238,000 miles from the Earth. This compares to Venus at twenty-four million miles at its closest proximity to Earth. A New Moon, represented by the conjunction of the Sun and Moon, occurs roughly once every month. It rotates around the Earth at 27.3 days. As both bodies are moving, the Moon's synodic cycle is roughly 29.5 days when measured from each New Moon to the next New Moon.

The placement of the Moon by sign and house is how we express our subjective emotional response to our environment. It symbolizes feminine and maternal energy, security and nurturing qualities. It stands for our emotional side, impulsiveness and instinctual feelings. It facilitates our growth of consciousness. The Moon is associated with our emotional and nurturing qualities. This is evident by the numerous idioms, expressions or words, related to the Moon. Phrases such as "being moonstruck", "over the moon", a lunatic, honeymoon, "once in a blue moon," etc.

MERCURY

Mercury is the closest planet to the Sun and rotates around the Sun in eighty-eight days. The Mercury-Earth conjunction occurs roughly every one hundred and sixteen days. As viewed from the Earth, Mercury is never more than 28 degrees from the Sun, so it is not surprising that it is the most common of the planetary conjunctions.

Mercury was named after the messenger of the gods. Astrologically speaking it represents communication, co-ordination and adaptability to our environment. Those with a Mercury conjunction benefit from clarity of mind and activity of the mind, intelligence and good reasoning abilities. It is through human intelligence, its curiosity and hunger for new knowledge and our ability to transfer its knowledge initially through writing and now over the internet and mass media that has differentiated us from other creatures of the animal kingdom. Mercury is the ruler of the zodiacal sign of Gemini and Virgo. Gemini is the sign of close and immediate relatives, and expression. Mercury also rules Virgo, the sign of discrimination and critical analysis.

VENUS

Like Mercury, Venus also revolves around the Sun within the orbit of the Earth. Venus takes roughly two hundred and twenty five earth days to make one complete revolution around the Sun. It is never more than forty-eight degrees from the Sun as viewed from the Earth. Next to the Moon it is the closest and brightest planet in the sky as the evening star.

Venus is associated with the feminine qualities of beauty, connectivity, and relationships. **It rules the sign of Taurus and Libra. Taurus is the sign of hard work and acquisition.** The beginning of the autumnal equinox is represented by the seventh sign of the zodiac, Libra. The daylight hours and night are equal thus Libra represents balance and harmony. I have been told that one key to success in life is to be in harmony with the universe. Certainly, there is some truth to the adage that states "a happy spouse is a happy house."

Venus represents harmony, the arts, and everything associated with luxury and beauty. It is common to find those with a strong Venus quality in artistic careers or in the beauty industry, modeling, florists, hair stylists, jewelry, confections, perfumes, handbags, beauty products, antiques and other luxury products.

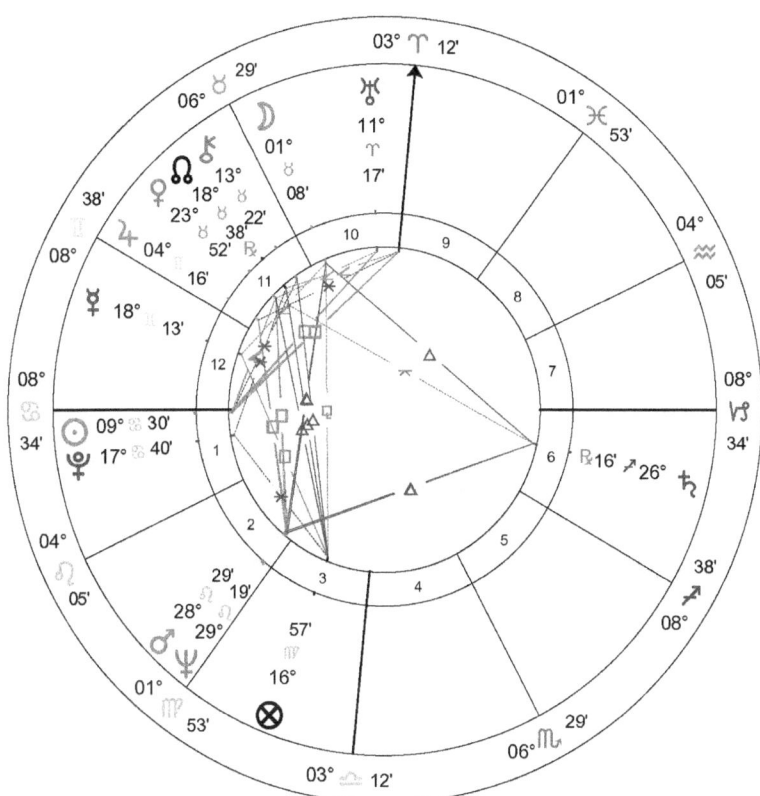

Natal Chart for Imelda Marcos, 07/02/1929, 05:30 AM, Manila, Philippines

Those who are well to do and have Venus in Taurus or Libra, often have a fondness for acquiring and collecting items such as art, real estate, jewelry, cars, antiques.

This brings to mind Imelda Marcos, who was married to Ferdinand Marcos, the president of the Philippines from 1965 to 1986. She has Mars conjunct Neptune as a Category I planetary conjunction. Her Category II special conjunction has her Sun in a partile conjunction to her Ascendant. As a double Cancer, she projects herself as a great hostess, and a warm and loving personality. As First Lady of the Philippines she was fully aware of her regal power and influence accentuated by Mars and Neptune in Leo. Her Venus, the ruler of Taurus, conjuncts her North Node in the eleventh house of hopes and desires. While their country endured economic hardship and civil war the couple lived a lavish and extravagant lifestyle.

Imelda was famous for her collection of some three thousand pairs of shoes of which some seven hundred are displayed in a museum.

It is unusual to find an affluent Taurus that doesn't have an interest in acquiring property or a collection of some sort. America is known for its car culture. Many male celebrities own expensive cars. Two famous celebrities, both noted for their classic car collections, that have their Sun in the sign of Taurus, are Jay Leno and Jerry Seinfeld.

MARS

Mars is the first planet beyond the orbit of the Earth. It rotates around the Sun about once every twenty-six months. Mars was closely associated with the God of War, as this red planet is covered with iron oxide dust. It is not unusual for those with a warrior spirit to be attracted to careers in sports, the military or law enforcement. It is represented by the qualities of a warrior. This includes martial spirit, physical energy, bravery, competitive spirit, drive, courage, assertiveness, and male sexual energy

Mars is the ruler of Aries, the first sign of the zodiac and spring. The first day of spring is the spring equinox, when the hours of daylight and night are equal at the equator. It is represented by the ram, as it runs headfirst to display its aggressiveness and strength.

Those with a planet conjunct Mars are independent, inspired and possess an independent spirit. They do not sit quietly but are actively engaged in their environment. They are physically active. In the movie business they find positions where they are involved in films requiring a lot of physical ability or action, such as stunt work. They are likely attracted to find work outdoors or as independent contractors rather than office work.

JUPITER

This planetary giant orbits the Sun beyond the asteroid belt and orbits the Sun once every twelve years. It is referred to as the greater benefic. It is associated with magnification, optimism, and benevolence. Jupiter rules the sign of Sagittarius, the sign of the higher mind, learning, travel, and expansion of consciousness through outer experiences. One of their positive features is having faith in oneself and the ability to be optimistic and confident in their outlook. Jupiter symbolizes expansion, growth and our belief system.

SATURN

This planet represents responsibility, discipline, hard work, external authority and the time-tested practices of tradition. Saturn represents the lessons of discipline and hard work. It is through patience and tenacity to overcome life's obstacles that you can achieve wisdom and success. In political astrology Saturn is associated with the institution of government, law and authority.

URANUS

This planet makes a complete revolution around the Sun every eighty-four years or seven years in each sign. This is the first of the trans-personal planets, or non-traditional planets. Uranus' orbit is not normal like others in that it is the only planet that revolves at nearly right angle to its orbit with a tilt of ninety-eight degrees. This leads to the eccentricity associated with the meaning of this planet.

Uranus rules the sign of Aquarius. It can stimulate intuition, creativity and insightfulness. Individuals with Uranus and Pluto conjunct their Part of Fortune, or their North Node to the axis points leave a very unique mark in the world. Those with a prominent Uranus conjunction are often known for their individuality. A person with strong Uranian qualities sees the normal process of reform too slow and more likely to support a revolutionary or unconventional approach. They are often a one of a kind, a rebel, unlike what we would expect from the "average" individual.

A person with a prominent Uranus can exhibit behavior in dramatic, inappropriate or disruptive behavior. When upset their reaction becomes apparent. Throwing a tantrum or getting angry with the potential of violence is not unusual. They may push as far as they can and get away with it unless stopped by some greater authority. This trait can be found in cult figures and politicians who appeal to the disaffected and those sick and tired of the status quo. Cult figures feed upon their exclusivity and their beliefs.

There are thousands of religions and cults worldwide and some cases have sparked violence. Just think of the Great Crusades, the Troubles, the sectarian conflict from 1968 – 1998 between Catholics in Northern Ireland and the Protestants. More recently we have conflicts in the Middle East. In addition to the established religions there are pseudo religions or cults, and a handful of them are radical enough to lead their followers to suffer the ultimate sacrifice. Their goal is to brainwash or manipulate their members psychologically to acquire power and/or monetary gain. Some have a predisposition for dominance and aggression which has led to the death of innocent civilians and even their own followers. Anyone with Uranus in a multiple conjunction especially with the North Node could be especially suspect of a cult following.

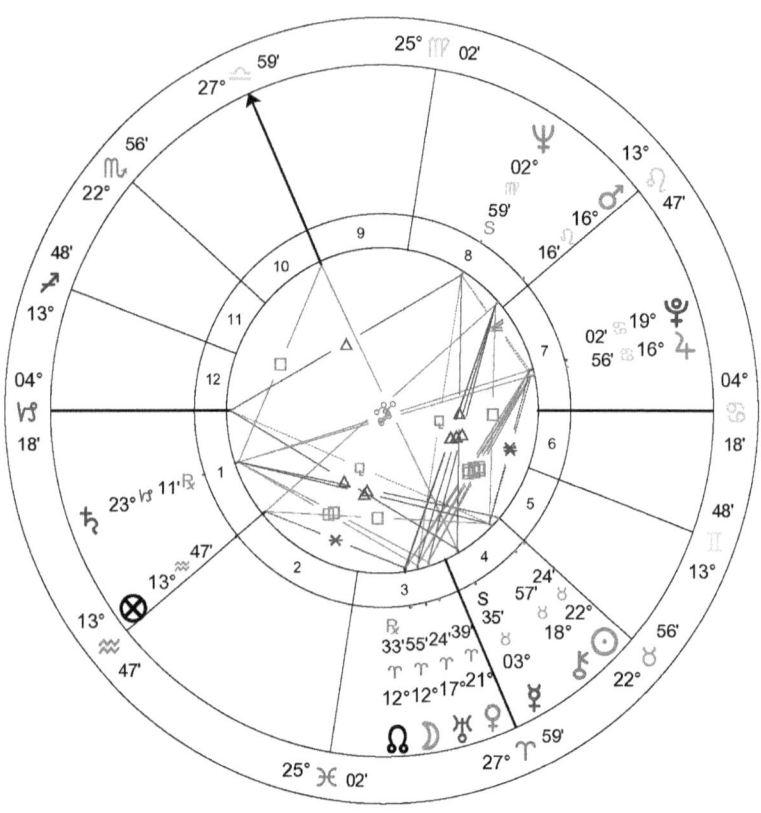

Natal Chart for Jim Jones, 05/13/1931, 10:00 PM, Lynn, Indiana

The above chart is for perhaps the most notorious of charismatic cult leaders, Jim Jones.

He led the People's Temple between 1955 -1978. In 1965 he moved his temple to California and became involved in political and charitable activities. In 1975 he established connections with prominent California politicians and was even appointed the chairman of the San Francisco Housing Authority Commission.

Following negative media publicity of abuses about his temple members, he ordered the construction of the Jonestown commune in Guyana. In November 1975, US Representative Leo Ryan led a delegation to the commune and tried to leave with some discontented temple followers. Congressman Ryan and four others were murdered by gunmen. Consequently, Jim Jones ordered the revolutionary mass murder-suicide of over nine hundred of its members including three hundred and four children.

Jim Jones has four Category I planetary conjunctions. His Moon is in a partile conjunction to his North Node, Uranus conjunct his North Node, Moon conjunct Uranus, and Jupiter conjunct Pluto. An astrologer would notice a cardinal T-Cross involving the outermost planets. It is composed of the opposition of Saturn to Jupiter and Pluto both in a difficult square aspect to Uranus. Jupiter conjunct Pluto. This can facilitate an association with greater calling, in this case a cult following. It can also facilitate great power and wealth. His Moon is in a partile conjunction to his North Node. It affects his emotional ability to radically influence his followers. He has no Category II special conjunctions. In the next chapter we shall see how the Sun conjunct Uranus and the North Node is manifested.

Name	Rodden Rating	Category I Planetary Conjunctions	Category II Special Conjunctions
Charles Manson (cult leader)	AA	Moon/NNode Mars/Neptune (P)	Jupiter/DSC PoF/IC
David Berkowitz (Son of Sam)	AA	Moon/NNode Mercury/Mars(P) Neptune/Saturn (P)	Moon/NNode/IC
Jim Jones (cult leader)	AA	Moon/NNode Moon/Uranus Jupiter/Pluto	
Marshall Applewhite (cult leader)	AA	Sun/Moon Jupiter/Pluto Uranus/NNode	PoF/ASC

Another cult leader was Marshall Applewhite, founder of the Heaven's Gate religious movement. He was responsible for the largest group suicide in the United Sates which claimed 39 lives. He has his Sun conjunct his Moon and Jupiter conjunct Pluto. Together with his North Node conjunct Uranus he was able to convince his followers to accept such a radical belief to leave their bodily "containers" to enter an alien spacecraft behind the comet Hale-Bopp.

Here is a partial list of cult leaders:

Name	Rodden Rating	Category I Planetary Conjunctions	Category II Special Conjunctions
Augusto Pinochet	AA	Moon/Saturn Uranus/NNode	
Jair Bolsonaro	AA	Jupiter/Uranus	Uranus/ASC
Nikolas Sarkozy	AA	Moon/Mars Jupiter/Uranus	Uranus/PoF
Viktor Orban	A	Mars/Uranus	

The planet Uranus is also prominent in the natal charts of a number of political figures.
- Augusto Pinochet, military dictator who ruled Chile from 1973-1990 has Uranus conjunct his North Node.
- Ayatollah Khomeini, (unknown birth time) has his North Node conjunct his Uranus.
- Barry Goldwater, politician, former major general in the Air Force Reserve, and US senator. His Sun is conjunct Mercury and Uranus. Mercury and Uranus form a partile conjunction.
- Donald Trump has a conjunction of Sun, Uranus, and his North Node.
- Jair Bolsonaro, president of Brazil (2019-2022) has Uranus conjunct his Ascendant.
- Nicholas Sarkozy (president of France in 2007 – 2012) has Uranus conjunct Jupiter and his Part of Fortune.
- Slobodan Milosevic (unknown birth time) has Saturn conjunct Uranus.
- Viktor Orban (prime minister of Hungary since 2010) has Mars conjunct Uranus.

Political leaders in foreign countries are not afraid to use the power of the state, violence or unorthodox measures to achieve their ends. In some third world countries some rise from the ranks of the military to gain political power. They are able to generate support from those who are discontented and those who blame the government for not representing their needs. Those with a prominent Uranus are strong proponents of change of the status quo. Once they seize power to attain their coveted position, they then must strive to maintain their position of power.

On a positive note, Uranus also embodies the qualities of innovation and inventors. Howard Hughes is one such example. Based on his birth date of December 24, 1905, he was born under three "Lucky Stars": Sun conjunct Uranus; Moon conjunct Venus and Mars conjunct Saturn. Many know him as an eccentric billionaire and his reclusive lifestyle in his later years. Few know that he was a businessman, aerospace engineer, pilot and inventor. He became prominent as a film director acquiring RKO studios and later became an important figure in aviation setting world air speed records and acquiring Trans World Airways (TWA). He was the founder of the Hughes Aircraft Company. He is also noted for his flying boat, the Spruce Goose. Other than its engines and electronics, it was made of wood and had the longest wingspan for any aircraft until 2019.

NEPTUNE

Neptune represents unconsciousness, dreams, visions and other intuitive qualities. Those having a "Lucky Star" connected with Neptune heightens their inspiration, creativity, and imagination. It adds to a person's emotional sensitivity and refinement of the arts. It also has to do with dreams, illusion and delusion. Many enjoy the excitement of their favorite sports team or action film heroes. That is why sports heroes and entertainers are paid so well.

Some people find a common outlet to escape the pain and daily grind by using drugs. Drugs and opioids have the anesthetic effects of Neptune clouding one's thought processes. It hides behind fantasy and illusion. Financially, Neptune is related to deception, scams and get rich schemes.

Modern technology has also given us flight simulators, special 3D movies, virtual reality, and video games to immerse us in a world of simulation and enhanced experience.

On the positive side, those with a prominent Neptune in their charts are often attracted to the arts and music.

As such, Neptune and Venus are associated with glamor, entertainment and the movie industry.

The spiritual world including religion, metaphysics, intuition, and dreams come under the domain of Neptune. Some seek solace in religion or maintain certain spiritual beliefs. Beyond Uranus is Neptune, the planet of individual/social consciousness and spirituality. The placement of Neptune symbolizes compassion and the dissolution of ego-consciousness. A prominent Neptune is present in the natal charts of highly evolved spiritual individuals.

This group of great spiritual leaders include Teilhard de Chardin, who has Neptune conjunct Venus, the 14th Dali Lama who has Neptune conjunct his Moon, Pope Paul II who has Neptune conjunct Jupiter and Paramahansa Yogananda who has Neptune conjunct Pluto. Each of them comes from different cultures and theological backgrounds and are recognized for their universal views. The Dali Lama and Archbishop Desmond Tutu, wrote "The Book of Joy: Lasting Happiness in a Changing World." They both faced oppression and exile but were able to maintain their sense of compassion.

PLUTO

Pluto has been declassified as a planet from the rest of the planetary family, known as our solar system, by the International Astronomical Union. Despite the fact it has five moons, it is now classified as a dwarf planet. However, Pluto continues to be recognized as a planet by astrologers and continues to be used in astrological interpretations.

Pluto was the mythological ruler of the underworld or Hades. Pluto is associated with life/death and the cycle of birth/rebirth. Together with Mars, the co-ruler of Scorpio, it is associated with life, legacies (inheritance), death, and sex. It is associated with sudden upheavals both positively and negatively. It symbolizes the power of regeneration, transformation and spiritual awareness.

Any planet conjunct Pluto can have a transformative effect upon an individual's life. It is the planet that goes beyond expectations, the need to explore life's deeper meanings of life, the super consciousness, the deeper meaning of life, or even the paranormal. In some cases, it has to do with the obsessive desire for change, upheaval, control and power struggles.

Together with other "Lucky Stars" this conjunction has the potential to have a massive transformative effect.

For example, when combined with Jupiter the person may be blessed with taking things to the extreme. It may indicate a dramatic change in consciousness or even in the possibility of considerable wealth.

CHAPTER THREE

PLANETARY COMBINATIONS

This chapter covers planetary pairs in a conjunction without regard to their sign and house placement. Conjunctions may be considered the spice of an astrological chart. A conjunction should not be viewed alone. One must also factor in the sign, house and if there are aspects to that conjunction.

SUN

Sun/Moon - When the Sun and Moon are conjunct in the same sign, you are considered a double (insert the Sun sign), and associate with qualities of that sign. Generally, such individuals have a close and positive parental relationship, are well adjusted, and have a good sense of Self. They are reasonably comfortable with themselves and act with self-assurance. They have a certain self-awareness in achieving their goals.

Sun/Mercury – This represents the creative power of the mind which sets us apart from all other species of the animal kingdom. This represents our ability to learn and indicates a good measure of intelligence, and our willingness to learn and transmit this knowledge to others. It includes our ability to express oneself with strong communication qualities. You enjoy intellectual stimulation and ideas. A person with this conjunction is likely to think things out rather than through one's emotions. Famous people with Sun partile Mercury include Wolfgang Amadeus Mozart.

Consider the house and sign in which Mercury and Sun are located. If it is in the sign of Leo, Gemini or Virgo it gives additional emphasis. For example, an individual with this conjunction in Gemini or Virgo may tend to talk and talk. A person with this combination in Virgo is known to write detailed journals. This planetary combination can be found in researchers, lecturers, teachers and writers.

I know of a woman who was a twin born just 40 minutes apart. They both shared the same sign for their Sun, Moon and Ascendant. They both had their Sun partile to Mercury in Virgo. When I spoke to the younger sister and explained the qualities of her Sun sign and the Sun being partile to Mercury she expressed that they more matched the qualities of her older sister. She told me her older sister had suffered from anorexia. The sixth house is related to work, health and service. Virgo is understandably the most common sign related to eating disorders. How was it that one woman suffered from an eating disorder and the other did not? Even though they shared the same Ascendant, the house divisions changed such that the older sister had Mercury as the ruler of her 6th house accentuating her health issue and accentuating the qualities of the Sun partile Mercury in Virgo.

Sun/Venus – You possess highly refined artistic qualities, refined, good taste, and an appreciation of quality and style. You express yourself in an affectionate manner and enjoy the company of people. You possess a strong ability to gain material wealth. Refer to the chapter on the Cazimi.

Sun/Mars – Generally a strong disposition, energetic, self-assertive, and outgoing. You are self-motivated and filled with drive but can be impulsive. You are more comfortable outdoors, and prefer dancing, swimming or running rather than passive activities.

Sun/Jupiter – Great for good fortune and wealth, generosity, advancement and recognition, enterprising, warm and approachable. You like to travel and learn about exotic lands and cultures. You are likely to expand your consciousness through exposure to new thoughts and philosophies.

Sun/Saturn – Generally the serious type, ability to focus and concentrate, magnanimous, strong advancement potential, hard worker, reserved and conservative. Individuals having this conjunction can firmly hold onto their convictions to support law and order. Individuals with this conjunction are likely to hold a conservative viewpoint and are resistant to change.

Sun/Uranus – Individuals with this conjunction often express an originality of appearance, thought and action. They may be viewed as bold, brash and ego eccentric. They may be viewed as revolutionary or radical rather than as activists or reformers. If they work within an institution such as the military or government, they may become whistle blowers. They may feel defensive when their views are challenged and a personal attack on their ego and pride and are likely to lash out. Some may hold a radical or revolutionary viewpoint. They can be very resistant to views other than their own. Some firmly hold onto certain unconventional thoughts, ideas and even conspiracy theories.

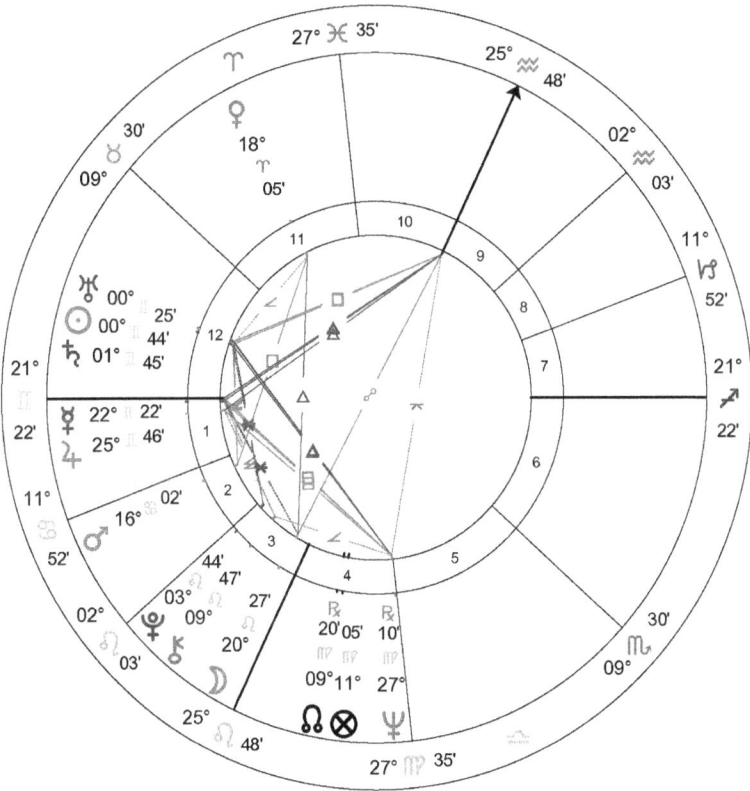

Natal Chart for Ted Kaczynski, 05/22/1942, 06:45 AM, Chicago, Illinois

A prime example of this planetary combination can be found in the chart of the person known as the "Unabomber", or Ted Kaczynski.

He was born May 22, 1942. He has his Sun, Saturn and Uranus within two degrees of each other. He has three Category I planetary conjunctions: Sun and Saturn, Sun and Uranus and Saturn and Uranus. His Sun is in a partile conjunction to his Uranus. The combination of Saturn and Uranus is a very difficult combination in that he has a strong rigid belief system and is firm in his convictions. A conjunction of Sun and Uranus is fraught with sudden change and can be explosive in nature. If we look at his astrological chart all three are within two degrees of each other in the sign of Gemini in the twelfth house of isolation and seclusion.

Kaczynski has two Category II conjunctions. One of them is Mercury in a partile conjunction to his Ascendant, indicative of a high degree of intelligence. He was highly educated and a gifted mathematician. He attended Harvard University and in 1969 became the youngest assistant professor at UC Berkeley.

A person's sense of character can be found by looking at the tightest aspect or conjunction in the chart. In his case, his Sun is in a partile conjunction to Uranus and also his Sun is nearly a partile conjunction to Saturn. In 1969 he dropped out of society and built a cabin in Montana.

He then set upon a seventeen-year (1978-1995) campaign of terror sending homemade bombs to scientists, businessmen and those who angered him. He once told an interviewer that "Ever since my early teens I had dreamed of escaping from civilization." He was a prolific writer (Mercury in a partile conjunction to his Gemini Ascendant). Mercury is the ruler of Gemini. He wrote a 35,000-word manifesto that he sent to the Washington Post and New York Times. When his cabin was raided by the FBI, they not only found bomb making materials but also 40,000 pages of a journal recording his daily life. For his Category II special conjunction, his Part of Fortune is conjunct his North Node which was overcome by the strength of his stellium. It may be indicative of what his destiny could have been had it been directed in a positive direction.

Interpretation of multiple independent variables, or planets, in a stellium can get more complicated as the number of variables increase. When there are two independent variables or two planets in a conjunction it usually involves a blended interpretation of the two planets. When there are three variables or planets, each possible combination needs to be considered. In a stellium of four variables there are six possible combinations. Vito Genovese has four planets within four degrees of each other.

With five independent variables/five planets increase to ten possible planetary combinations. Lucky Luciano has five planets all within four degrees. When this situation occurs try to find the dominant planetary conjunction. This can often be done by looking for a partile aspect within the grouping of planets or seeing if one of the planets is the natural ruler of that sign.

Name	RR	Category I Conjunctions by Sign/Degree/Minute	Category II Planetary Conjunctions	Special Conjunctions
Chelsea Manning	X	Merc 22 Sag 08 Saturn 23 Sag 47 Sun 25 Sag 15 Uranus 26 Sag 48 **Moon** 15 Scorp 13 **Mars** 15 Scorp 30	Sun/Mercury Sun/Saturn Sun/Uranus Moon/Mars	
Daniel Ellsberg	AA	**NNode** 14 Aries 22 **Uranus** 15 Aries 25 Sun 16 Aries 52	Sun/NNode Uran/NNode Sun/Uranus	Venus/PoF PoF/MC
Donald Trump	AA	Uran 17 Gemini 54 NNode 20 Gemini 48 Sun 22 Gemini 56	Sun/Uranus Sun/NNode Uran/NNode	Mars/ASC
Vito Genovese	AA	Sun 29 Scorpio 10 **Mars** 29 Scorp 16 **Uranus** 29 Scorp 18 Saturn 2 Sagittarius 50	Sun/Mars (P) Sun/Uran (P) Mars/Uran (P)	
Lucky Luciano	AA	Uranus 29 Scorp 31 Mars 1 Sag 36 Sun 2 Sag 29 **Saturn** 3 Sagittarius 13 **Moon** 3 Sag 28	Sun/Moon (P) Sun/Mars (P) Sun/Sat (P) Sun/Uranus Moon/Sat (P) Mars/ Saturn Mars/Uranus	PoF/ASC (P) Sun/Saturn/ Moon/MC
Ted Kaczynski	AA	**Uran** 0 Gemini 26 **Sun** 0 Gemini 45 Sat 1 Gemini 46	Sun/Saturn Sun/Uran (P) Saturn/Uranus	Merc/ASC(P) NNode/PoF

Listed above we have an interesting group of individuals where the principal planets involve the Sun and Uranus. Since they are within a stellium I have identified them by degree and minute.

In the list of names above I highlighted in bold type the tightest aspect in the chart, or a partile conjunction. What if there are not any planetary conjunctions? In that case look for the tightest aspect in the chart.

Lucky Stars, Lucky Life

Try extending the search for any partile aspects to other planets by major aspect, (trine, square or opposition), to the Part of Fortune, North Node, Ascendant, MC, Descendant or IC.

Chelsea Manning's chart has a stellium. It includes her Sun and three planets in Sagittarius but there are no partile conjunctions. It appears she has a couple of issues. The first issue has to do with her Sun conjunct Uranus and Saturn might bring up thoughts of rebellious behavior against authority/military (Saturn). The second issue appears to be an emotional issue as the tightest aspect is actually a partile aspect of her Moon (15 Scorpio 13) and Mars (15 Scorpio 30). There is only a separation of 17 minutes to an exact conjunction. A closer look shows that this partile conjunction is in the sign of Scorpio ruled by Mars. She may have been influenced by deep emotional reasons to obtain and release classified government documents through WikiLeaks.

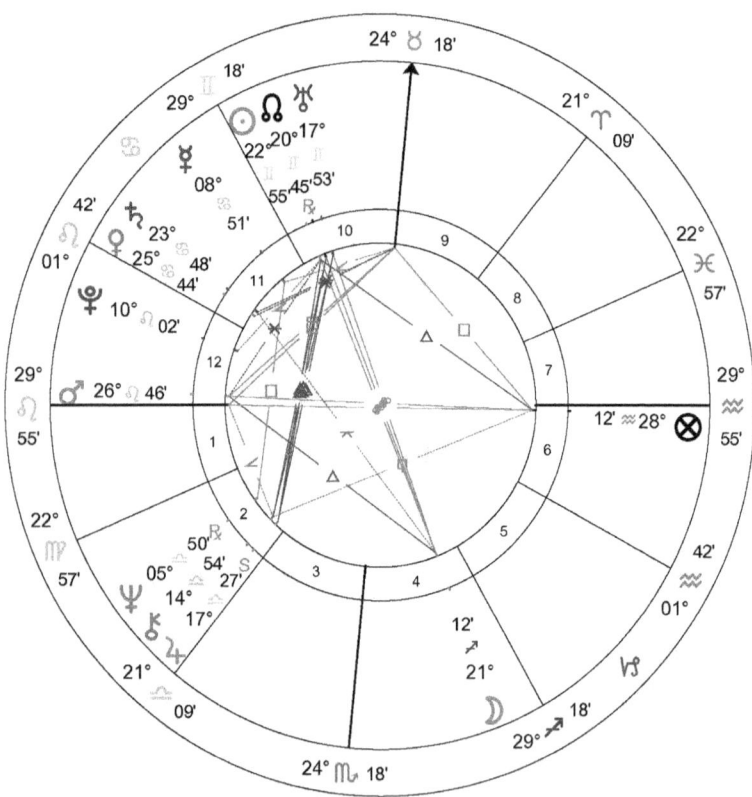

Natal Chart for Donald Trump, 06/14/1946, 10:54 AM, Queens, New York

Donald Trump is constantly in the daily news. His chart has four Category I conjunctions. His Sun is conjunct Uranus, Sun conjunct his North Node, Uranus conjunct his North Node and Venus conjunct Saturn. His Category II special conjunction has his Part of Fortune conjunct his Descendant.

There has been no other US president quite like him. This is because his Sun is conjunct both his Uranus and North Node. Having his Sun in opposition to his Moon shows that he was born under a Full Moon. With his Sun conjunct his North Node, he is the only US president born under a lunar eclipse.

He has no partile conjunctions in his chart. If we look for the tightest major aspect, we discover that Jupiter (17 Libra 27) and Uranus (17 Gemini 53) are just 26 minutes to an exact trine. This trine shows just how "lucky" he is. It is possible that with his luck and his well-placed Part of Fortune, he may have his convictions overturned and not serve any prison time.

He is able to take full advantage of the power of the Sun, North Node and Uranus in Gemini and Mars on his Ascendant in the outrageous statements he makes, often with little regard for the truth. There are numerous examples but one that was repeated over and over was the "stolen election" that led to his supporters to attack the US Capitol Building on January 6, 2021.

With his Sun, North Node and Uranus, in the tenth house of recognition, trine to Jupiter, in his second house of personal resources, it shows he is an opportunist to promote himself and enrich himself. For example, within two days of the verdict of being guilty on thirty-four felony counts, Donald Trump reached out to his supporters and was able to raise over $70 million to help fund his election campaign and his legal fees.

Sun/Neptune – This combination brings sensitivity to other worldly influences and susceptibility to alcohol and drugs. It also helps one to express one's artistic qualities and attract people to a creative profession such as acting. Acting involves portraying oneself in character to fit the role within the script. Such a person can be distracted from reality and be lost in a world of fantasy or a utopian vision.

Although we don't have his birth time, Eric Arthur Blair, author, novelist and political commentator, was better known under his pen name, George Orwell. He was the author of "Animal Farm" and "Nineteen Eighty-Four." Both are science fiction and dystopian novels characterized by fear, distress, and tyrannical rule. He has three Category I planetary conjunctions with Sun, Moon and Neptune all within two degrees of each other strongly stimulating his imagination. He also has Mars four degrees from his North Node.

Sun/Pluto – Potential for greatness yet forceful, intense, potential for greatness, likely to accept social reforms and changes, likely to act in the extreme.

Sun or Moon to the North Node – Driven by an inner sense of individual purpose or destiny.

Sun/Ascendant – If the Sun appears in the first house it closely relates to physical appearance. If the Sun is in the first house the person would have an energetic, strong personality, self-confident, generally popular, affable, desire for recognition. Often a sunny and charming disposition.

Sun/MC – Very fortunate. Recognition of fame and achievements.

MOON

Within a period of less than thirty days, the Moon completes its orbit around the earth and in doing so travels through each sign of the zodiac. Therefore, it is the most commonly occurring conjunction. I once met three people within a period of two weeks who had either a Moon-Pluto conjunction or Moon-Pluto opposition.

Moon/Mercury – This is a combination of emotion and the intellect. A good mind, studious, and the ability to stay focused. Those who have this combination make good poets, writers, songwriters, and able to intellectually and emotionally appeal to others.

Moon/Venus – Sociable, affable, affectionate, attractive, relatable, popular, talented.

Moon/Mars – Strong vitality, able to take charge and command, energetic and assertive.

Moon/Jupiter – Generous, successful, sensitive to other people's feelings, warm, and popular.

Moon/Saturn – Patient, serious, respectful, restrained in expression of feelings, industrious, practical.

Moon/Uranus – Indicates a willingness to accept new and original ideas including unusual interests. There is a strong passion to solve and explore new ideas. Unconventional. It brings forth the intuitive and innovative qualities very often found in individuals who are artistic and creative. An excellent example it the Danish physicist Niels Bohr known for his dedication, hard work and creative work on quantum mechanics during WWII. He was recognized with the Nobel Prize for his contribution to the Manhattan Project. His Category I planetary conjunctions include his Moon conjunct Mercury, and Moon in a partile conjunction to Uranus. He also has his North Node conjunct Jupiter which aided in his recognition.

Moon/Neptune – Very sensitive, intuitive, altruistic, psychic, passionate, artistic and likely has some hidden talent. This gives the ability to express one's subtle and individual touch in their talent. Talent can be expressed through emotions in art, dance, music or acting.

The manifestation of "Lucky Stars" are not limited to Hollywood stars and other famous people. For example, recently during lunch I spoke to a proud father who talked about his daughter's involvement in the Japanese anime entertainment industry. Curious, I asked for her birth date. I then looked up the planets on an ephemeris. I was surprised to find she was born during a tight conjunction of her Sun (9 Capricorn 02), Moon (7 Capricorn 7) and Neptune (5 Capricorn 39). She is a double Capricorn being born during the New Moon. There are three Category I planetary conjunctions consisting of her Sun and Moon, Moon and Neptune and Sun and Neptune. Glamor, fantasy, animation, gaming, movies, and the entertainment industry fall under the archetype of Neptune.

When this talented American is not teaching music to young kids, Stephanie Yanez has found her passion as a J-pop music artist. She is also an author, a model, singer and performer. She sings in both Japanese and English and has released several albums. She has appeared in several anime venues and has performed in Japan and the United States. Her fascination in Japanese anime has grown from a fan of Sailor Moon, to winning the AX Idol at Anime Expo and she has even gone on tour. She makes appearances at various anime events and conventions in Southern California. Through various connections and opportunities in the Japanese recording industry she looks forward to new and exciting projects.

Moon/Pluto – This combination can have an extremely deep emotional outlook leading to a very dramatic emotional life. You may experience extremes in your feelings and dark moods. This powerful combination gives you the ability to influence the outcome of your life. You have the desire to gain an important position of authority.

For example, Wolfgang Amadeus Mozart, was a popular and prolific composer who wrote over eight hundred works. He not only has Sun partile his Mercury but also the exact conjunction of his Moon and

Pluto. He rose in influence as a court musician finally obtaining an aristocratic patronage as chamber composer under Emperor Joseph II. He lived a life of extravagance but died in poverty at the age of thirty-five.

The power and influence of Moon/Pluto may not guarantee you fame but you may hold positions of importance such as being board member in your homeowner's association, city council, or other positions of greater power and influence. You are especially sensitive to social conditions and social injustices and may make a great effort to bring about improved conditions in your environment. Since this conjunction involves the influence of Pluto it can also broaden metaphysical or religious issues. Famous people born with Sun conjunct Pluto include Katy Perry, Emma Stone, Elizabeth Kubler-Ross, and Padre Pio.

Moon/Ascendant – Feelings are a strong part of one's personality, emotions are a strong quality and able to strongly relate to others.

Moon/MC – Success achieved through a strong sense of emotional commitment.

MERCURY

Mercury/Venus – Strong musical and artistic talent. People with this combination have a strong urge to communicate with others. They can make excellent authors, romance novelists, journalists, editors, and script writers.

Mercury/Mars – A person with this combination can communicate directly if not forcefully with confidence. It would depend upon what sign or element this conjunction occurs. The individual can be logical and practical. They are likely to be good at verbal arguments and quick in rebuttals. This quality makes for a good debater or lawyer.

Mercury/Jupiter – Open to new ideas, philosophical, willing to learn, and adaptable to new ideas. Is willing to ask questions for the sake of knowledge. You are both intelligent and sociable and thus able to get along with most people. You are able to weave logic and analysis in your thoughts to others. You have excellent ability to convey your thoughts and ideas to others. It can be found in writers, motivational speakers, and those in marketing and sales.

Mercury/Saturn – Someone who is very focused, logical, structured, and analytical. It reflects a serious and disciplined mind capable of critical analysis. Such a person is comfortable in a career that is highly structured such as an accountant, manager, mathematician, statistician, or even a philosopher.

They tend to lean toward a strict conservative viewpoint. In a traditional sense, they could also be a researcher, religious leader or even a politician. They should be careful not to be overly critical of others.

Mercury/Uranus – An individual with this combination is open to new ideas and can display a willingness to try a new and novel approach in problem solving. It indicates a person who breaks from tradition (Saturn) to be an innovator, designer, and trend setter. This combination reflects a bright mind able to solve difficult puzzles or problems.

Technology is advancing so quickly that colleges and universities are offering degrees that did not exist forty years ago. This includes video game development, podcasting, quantum computing, artificial intelligence, robotics, etc. Technology that was cutting edge for the baby boomers is commonplace for the Gen X and millennials.

Mercury/Neptune - Diffuses mental facilities, and promotes imagination, and artistic qualities. You possess a visionary mind beyond simple facts and figures. There is a good balance between being book smart and being in a world that could use greater understanding and compassion. You can find yourself having an interest in science fiction, dystopian or zombie themes. You have strong intuitive and creative abilities in a field helping others.

The German monk and theologian who inspired the Protestant reformation, Martin Luther, has the exact conjunction of Mercury and Neptune (religion) and a partile conjunction of Venus and Saturn.

Mercury/Pluto – Indicates a powerful intellect, excellent communication skills, and open to new thoughts and ideas. You have the ability to think outside the box and perceive what some might think of as the impossible. This combination stimulates the mind to new ideas and opportunities and is visionary in one's thinking. Mark Zuckerberg, who created Facebook, created a revolutionary approach in social media, has Mercury within one degree of an exact opposition to Pluto.

Mercury/Ascendant – You portray yourself as an intelligent person, able to express yourself well, a good communicator. Having an active mind, you can be quite talkative and expressive. This is a good quality to express yourself through writing, screen writing, lecturing, teaching, as well as stand up performances.

Mercury/MC – Able to achieve success through expressive communication. It can be as an actor or in an academic field.

VENUS

Venus/Mars – On a personal level there is a strong drive between the female sensuality of Venus and male passion of Mars. An individual with this conjunction is demonstrative, emotionally expressive, and passionate in their life and work. Look for aspects to this conjunction to see how this intense energy is released.

Venus/Jupiter – Warm personality, optimistic, expressive in their actions and emotions.

Venus/Saturn – Emotionally reserved, loyal, modest and focused on one's career. May indicate a sense of isolation and delay in forming close relationships. In extreme cases it may indicate issues with a father figure or authority.

Venus/Uranus – You can be highly romantic, very talented, gifted, yet a desire for freedom and independence. You have an eccentric appeal about you. You are likely endowed with great looks or beauty. If you are the dating type, you may find it difficult to form a committed relationship if you have this planetary combination.

Venus/Neptune – Very refined tastes, devoted, sensual, idealistic, empathy, compassionate, highly intuitive. Be careful not to be seduced into what appears to be an ideal relationship as well. Celebrities with this conjunction include Gina Lollobrigida, Sophia Loren, Meg Ryan, and Richard Gere.

This planetary combination attracts dancers, painters, musicians, and artists. In their spare time they may be attracted to video games. It attracts those into the movie industry both in front and behind the camera. Many find careers involved in the beauty industry which include modeling, jewelry, antiques, haute cuisine, photography, cosmetics, jewelry, antiques, and even real estate.

Venus/Pluto – With Pluto this takes the qualities of Venus to a higher level. You can be altruistic and devote your interests to humanitarian, environmental or animal causes. You seek a deeper understanding of life on a spiritual level than simply casual physical relationships. You may also be attracted to seeking and understanding the universe, not through conventional religion or philosophy, but non-traditional approach such as the paranormal or metaphysics.

Venus/Ascendant – Refined, warm personality, and very attractive.

Venus/MC – As the MC represents one's public image, career and achievements; Venus conjunct the MC enjoys a favorable position. It embraces a person of talent and aesthetic quality.

MARS

Mars/Jupiter – Anyone with this combination shows great entrepreneurial spirit and a willingness to direct energies to new projects. Such a person is resourceful, optimistic, and is confident. Unlike the introvert, you love the outdoors and social events. You are likely to do well in sports, acting, and areas where you can express your creative talents drawing public attention to your talents.

Mars/Saturn – People with this combination are able to focus their energies and are hard working. You are self-assured in your actions, and able to able to focus on long term rewards. You have the drive and determination to overcome obstacles combined with a strong work ethic.

Mars/Uranus – This combination demonstrates a willingness to be fearless, take risks to the point of violence, and accept revolutionary ideas. You may be impulsive and have volatile tendencies. Example: Angela Davis, who was a political activist, was involved in the far left as a member of the Communist Party of the USA, Student Non-Violent Coordinating Committee and the Black Panther movement. She has Mars conjunct Uranus, Sun opposed to Pluto which is conjunct her North Node. Angela has since channeled the rebellious energies of her youth to become an author, lecturer and a professor and activist supporting certain social causes.

Mars/Neptune – Can be penetrating and aggressive in exploring new ideas. Mars stimulates the imagination and artistic qualities. You may be passionate about your views.

Mars/Pluto – Stimulates strong emotional energies, can be impulsive and temperamental. When poorly aspected, Mars and Pluto can be expressed in violence.

Mars/Ascendant – Indicative of a strong and forceful dynamic personality. One who is very outgoing and is quite physical and energetic. Athletically inclined, seeks a physical outlet such as a regular workout at the gym or exercise to release this pent-up energy. This individual has lots of energy to accomplish their goals.

Mars/MC – Able to reach their success through a strong sense of drive and energy.

JUPITER

Jupiter/Saturn – These are two social or planetary giants and the furthest visible planets. These individuals are organized and focused, possessing strong determination to achieve their goals. They often exhibit strong leadership and management/executive abilities and fit well in a large organization. They often hold management positions. If you have this conjunction aspect you have the courage, determination, and ambition to be successful in your career. Walt Disney had a Jupiter/Saturn conjunction.

Jupiter/Uranus – Freedom loving, inspirational, resourceful, ability to adapt to new ideas and situations.

Jupiter/Neptune – Conjunctions between the outer planets occur less frequently as they are slower moving. The last time a Jupiter/Neptune conjunction occurred was between May and August 2009. A person born with this combination is likely to be devoted, generous and idealistic. This planetary combination can heighten one's psychic and emotional sensitivity. It is an excellent combination for artists and musicians who have a willingness to explore different mediums and techniques. It can also lead to interests in paranormal and metaphysics.

Neptune was the ruler of the sea so there is a strong affinity for the sea and liquids. There can be an interest in conservation and environmentalism. I know of a lady who has a prominent Neptune in her chart and when she was much younger was an excellent swimmer, served as a lifeguard. She also teaches painting and is a professional artist, painting ocean scenes. This combination is likely to attract individuals in the film industry or even in artificial intelligence where imagination holds no bounds.

Jupiter/Pluto – The conjunction of Jupiter and Pluto occurs in intervals of twelve to thirteen years. The most recent Jupiter/Pluto conjunction happened in December 2007 and then again in April 2020.

This is one of the most beneficial planetary combinations. Individuals with this conjunction aspire to achieve greatness and to leave a mark in the world. Such an individual has enormous drive and ambition to achieve their greatness. They can be successful in whatever field they choose. Bill Gates, the founder and head of Microsoft, billionaire and philanthropist has Jupiter, representing abundance and generosity, in a partile conjunction to Pluto.

Jupiter/Ascendant – Expresses an aura of charm and warm personality. Has a positive outlook about oneself and life.

Jupiter/MC – Often a sign of great wealth by achieving the peak of one's career and recognition for their work and ambition.

SATURN

Saturn/Uranus – Uranus can be thought of a higher octave of Mercury. The combination of Saturn and Uranus makes you highly self-aware of the existing limits of traditional thinking which may result in you seeking a revolutionary perspective or ideas. It involves breaking existing institutional or philosophical barriers. This fresh perspective can be in the form of a revolutionary political theory, or even a religious outlook. Through hard work and discipline such a person should be able to achieve success in their unique field. The result may be a radical approach.

Both Paul Simon and Art Garfunkel were born in 1941 when Saturn and Uranus were retrograde and conjunct. They met each other in elementary school and became famous as one of America's great folk singer duos.

Saturn/Neptune – Saturn symbolizes discipline, structure, and limitation. Neptune represents spirituality, dreams and imagination. This conjunction can create tension or uncertainty between reality and escapism. The cycle of Saturn and Neptune is roughly every thirty-five to thirty-seven years.

Conjunctions are one of the most important aspects used in transits and other forecasting tools. Transits are when the planets of a particular day cross planets or key points in your in the natal or event chart by forming a major aspect to it.

Saturn/Pluto – This conjunction occurs every thirty-three to thirty-eight years, due to Pluto's elliptical orbit.

The last Saturn/Pluto conjunction occurred between early 2019 and was exact in January 2020 during the COVID-19 epidemic. This conjunction can be associated with hardships. Those with this conjunction can be firm in their convictions and ideals, tenacious to the point of being defiant of existing norms, looking for opportunities that are not orthodox. Able to keep on pushing and break new barriers.

Saturn/Ascendant – The consummate professional, serious, no nonsense, very responsible and dedicated to their craft. May appear aloof and not easily approachable.

Saturn/MC – Achievement and honors received for their hard work and leadership qualities. Saturn is the ruler of the tenth sign of the zodiac, Capricorn. They are often good managers as they take their roles seriously with a sense of duty and commitment. They hold positions of authority and are often executives. They take their positions seriously and are responsible leaders. This combination can be found in positions of state executive roles such as Justin Trudeau, Helmut Kohl, Kamala Harris and Queen Elizabeth II.

URANUS

Uranus/Neptune – This conjunction is quite rare occurring once in one hundred and sixty-eight years. Ability to explore and share creative ideas, aspiring, able to create a unique performance.

This rare conjunction gives the ability to inspire future generations unbounded by existing traditions and beliefs. Let's look at how it affected the life of an individual of an earlier Uranus/Neptune conjunction.

Susan B. Anthony was born February 15, 1820 (birth time unknown). She was a writer, a civil rights activist, and a strong advocate of women's rights. She has five Category I planetary conjunctions. As a reformer she has Uranus (27 Sagittarius 54) conjunct Neptune (0 Sagittarius 17). Her Sun (25 Aquarius 59) is conjunct Jupiter (28 Aquarius 52) are both in the progressive sign of Aquarius. She also has Venus (26 Pisces 35) in a partile conjunction to Pluto (26 Pisces 20). Both Venus and Pluto are conjunct Saturn (29 Aries 01). Her Saturn (29 Pisces 01) is conjunct her North Node (2 Aries 18).

She was destined to be a fighter for the progressive movement. She fought for equal rights for women including the rights for women to own property, equal pay, and played a pivotal role in the women's suffrage movement. Though her efforts and that of her supporters, the way was eventually paved for the 19th Amendment which gave women the right to vote.

Whenever planets are situated at critical degrees at the end or beginning of the sign it can be very significant. One example of planets on critical degrees can be found in the chart of Mary Baker Eddy, born July 16, 1821. She was a Christian healer, religious teacher and founder of the Christian Science movement. She was born when Uranus (0 Capricorn 12) was partile Neptune (1 Capricorn 5). While this is significant, this conjunction was strongly influenced by a square aspect to Pluto (29 Pisces 49), also at a critical degree.

Just as Uranus is a higher octave of Mercury, Neptune is a higher octave of Venus. The influence of these two planets works on the subconscious level. This planetary combination in a natal chart can be a very powerful influence and a potential career in the lucrative entertainment field. This combination in the sign of Capricorn, that of hard-working successful performers. They include singers, songwriters, and performers such as Miley Cyrus, Justin Bieber, Nick Jonas and Selena Gomez.

The most recent alignment of Uranus-Neptune was 1993. It will be interesting to see how the conjunction of Uranus and Neptune works as Saturn in Aquarius is square Pluto in Scorpio.

Uranus/Pluto – The last Uranus/Pluto conjunction was October 1965 and June 1966. These two generational, outer planets are linked to social upheaval. This period was marked by the civil rights movement, Vietnam War, anti-war protests, counter cultural movements, and political assassinations. This conjunction occurs roughly once every one hundred and ten to one hundred and thirty years. This planetary cycle is not as regular as other planetary cycles as the orbit of Pluto is elliptical.

Uranus/Ascendant – Individuals born under this combination have a unique, extraordinary quality to their appearance. Uranus is the ruler of Aquarius and as such these individuals are independent, freedom loving, unconventional, and often hold strong convictions. These people may not dress conventionally. Some wear tattoos and piercings to garner the attention of others and may attract others who may not understand them.

Uranus/MC – Able to achieve success through their unique ideals, creativity and unconventional concepts coming from a strongly independent person. In a transit it can indicate a sudden and stressful change or violent change in one's career or public profile.

NEPTUNE

Neptune/Pluto – This conjunction occurs roughly once every four hundred and ninety years. The last time it occurred was in 1891-1892. Ability to absorb heightened sensitivity to the extreme. This is a powerful transformative aspect between our belief systems, spiritual, mystical, and creative quality of Neptune. When combined with Pluto there may be an obsessive desire of renewal, rebirth or new beginnings.

J.R.R Tolkien, the author of "The Hobbit" and "Lord of the Rings" was attracted to a world rich in fantasy. He was born January 3, 1892, in South Africa.

He has Neptune strongly influencing imagination (8 Gemini 45) in a partile conjunction to Pluto (7 Gemini 15). Both planets are retrograde in the sign of Gemini (writing). He also had the benefit of two planets on critical degrees, Saturn (0 Libra 7) square Mercury (0 Capricorn 5).

Another example is the chart of George Adamski, philosopher, teacher and early UFO researcher. He was born April 17, 1891, with a Rodden Rating A. He was born with Neptune (5 Gemini 3), conjunct Pluto (6 Gemini 28) also conjunct his North Node (6 Gemini 11).

Neptune/Ascendant – A personality driven by their unique sense of self that few can understand. They are sensitive to others and can be quite intuitive.

Neptune/MC - Ability to achieve success through their ability to be sensitive. Many successful people can be found in the glamor, entertainment and movie industry.

PLUTO

Pluto/Ascendant – A strong sense of inner power that will manifest in great success.

Pluto/MC – Culmination of one's life through an intense desire to be recognized by society, sometimes in an unconventional manner. For example, Oscar Pistorius, the South African sprint runner was controversial as the first amputee to compete in an Olympic track event using a revolutionary blade runner prosthesis. His Category I planetary conjunctions include Pluto conjunct his MC and Venus conjunct Pluto. Tragically he was convicted in the murder of his girlfriend who was a model.

CHAPTER FOUR

THE CAZIMI

Of the numerous planetary combinations there is one special conjunction that most stands out to manifest the success features of "Lucky Stars, Lucky Life." This special "Lucky Star" is an exact conjunction of the Sun and Venus, known as a cazimi. In this chapter I will dive a little deeper to explain the features of those born under this unique "Lucky Star."

What is a cazimi? Simply speaking, the cazimi is an Arabian astronomical term, literally means "in the heart of the Sun." According to Arabic and medieval astrologers, a cazimi is any planet whose center is within 17 minutes of arc to the Sun. According to ancient Arabic astrologers it is considered a most auspicious aspect associated with great luck and opportunity.

There is a certain personality, sociability, and charisma that enables those with this cazimi to connect with others. The cazimi possesses the values and virtues of the planet Venus such as self-esteem and financial matters. Venus rules the signs of Taurus and Libra. The sign of Taurus is associated with persistence, hard work and the accumulation of wealth. Libra is associated with harmony, love, beauty, and sociability.

Those having a conjunction of the Sun and Venus generally possess both creative ability as well as an appreciation of the arts, music, harmony, and justice.

Let's not forget that the symbol of Libra is represented by the scales of justice.

Venus passes between the earth and Sun about once every nineteen months. There are two unique features about the cazimi of the Sun and Venus in the charts of the showcased individuals. First, the individuals that are highlighted in this chapter all happen to be born during the superior conjunction phase of the Sun and Venus. Mercury and Venus revolve around the Sun within the orbit of the Earth. When their conjunctions cross in front of the Sun it is an inferior conjunction and when behind the Sun it is a superior conjunction.

Not just any Sun cazmi Venus ensures fame and fortune. In addition to the Sun/Venus cazimi, each individual requires the dynamic and purposeful energies of an opposition aspect in their chart; the second most powerful aspect in astrology. An opposition of two planets can be found where two or more planets are separated by 180 degrees. The significance of the opposition is that it serves as a psychological connection to the opposite hemisphere, sign and house. An opposition in a chart is thought to involves some sort of tension, stress or uneasiness requiring resolution.

The Sun/Venus cycle has an interesting periodic cycle. Venus is known for its eight-year cycle stemming from the fact that thirteen Venusian orbits are very nearly equal to eight Earth years. Many astrologers know this as the pentagram or eight petals of Venus. As such, Venus tends to reappear in the same place forming a conjunction on or about the same date every eight years. In the study of solar returns this tends to give the added boost of the natal Sun/Venus cazimi every eight years which makes this cazimi unique among all the other planetary conjunctions.

The first person I would like to cover that was born with the Sun cazimi Venus is Leona Helmsley. She was born July 4, 1920, at 6:00 am in Marbletown, NY. She was a real estate mogul owning over 100 hotels and properties mostly in New York City and rose to fame in the 1980s. She and her husband even bought the Empire State Building.

Leona has three Category I "Lucky Stars" - the cazimi of the Sun and Venus: Sun conjunct Pluto, and Mercury conjunct Neptune. There are no Category II conjunctions. The tightest aspect is the sextile between Saturn and Pluto. It shows a possible personality of control and domination.

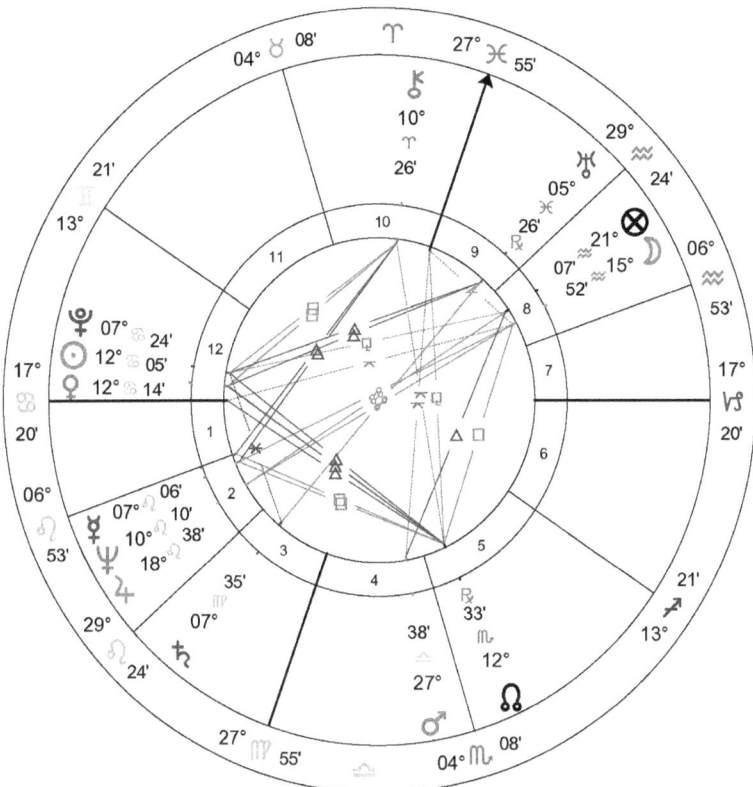

Natal Chart of Leone Helmsley, 07/04/1920, 06:00 AM, Marbletown, New York

Leona was known for her arrogant and offensive personality and referred to as the "Queen of Mean." She evaded taxes and was known for saying that "only the little people pay taxes." She was charged with defrauding stockholders and eventually found guilty of tax fraud and served time in prison. On a positive note, their trust is a global philanthropy with an endowment of $8 billion.

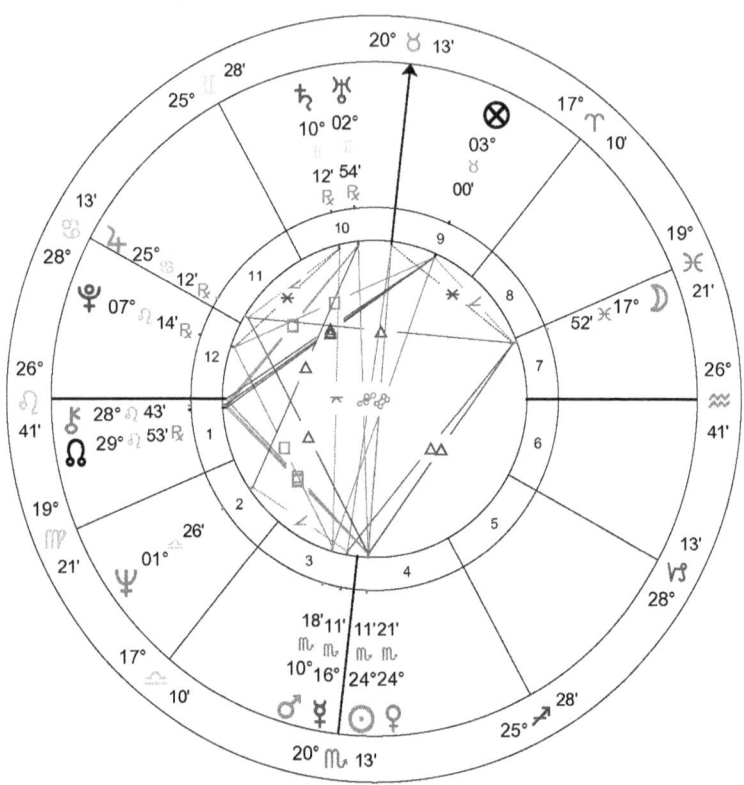

Natal Chart of Martin Scorsese, 11/17/1942, 12:24 AM, Flushing, New York

The next featured celebrity is the noted film director, producer and screenwriter, Martin Scorsese.

Martin Scorsese was born with his Sun (24 Scorpio 12) cazimi to his Venus (24 Scorpio 22). It is noteworthy that the ruler of his Leo Ascendant, the Sun (24 Scorpio 12), and the ruler of this tenth house, Taurus, Venus, conjunct his IC. Other Category II conjunctions include Mercury, four degrees from his IC, the cazimi of Sun and Venus also four degrees to his IC and his North Node four degrees from his Ascendant.

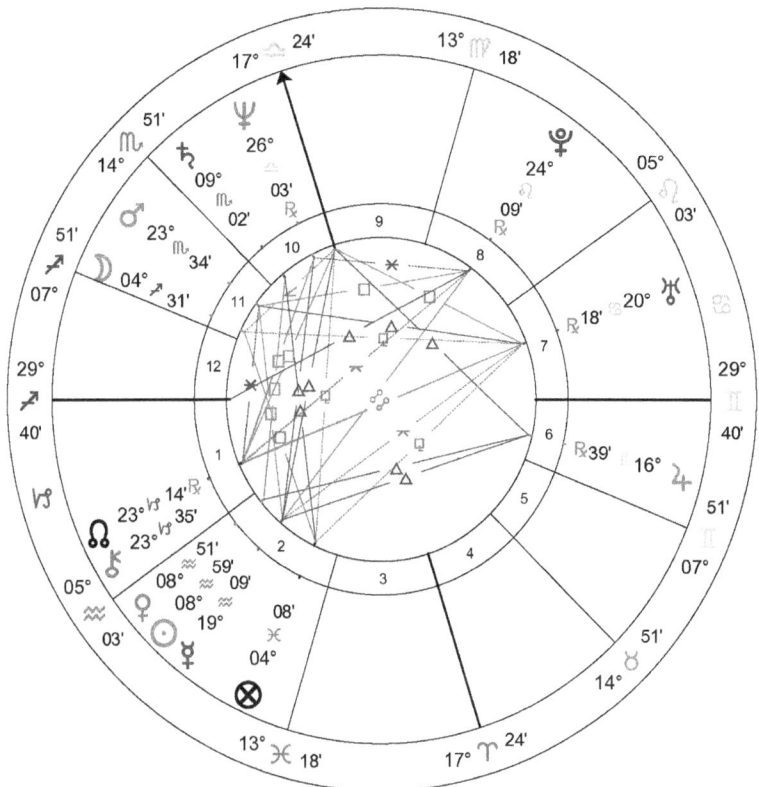

Natal Chart of Oprah Winfrey, 01/29/1954, 04:30 AM, Kosciusko, Mississippi

The next person born with a cazimi of the Sun and Venus is that of Oprah Winfrey, actress, media executive, talk show host, producer and philanthropist.

Oprah's chart has a Rodden Rating of "A" being born at 4:30 am. Other than the Sun/Venus cazimi she does not have any planetary conjunctions and non-planetary special conjunctions. However, she has two impressive Air Grand Trines. I would discount the influence on her MC since she has a Rodden Rating A.

The tightest aspect in her chart is not the cazimi of Sun and Venus but Sun (9 Aquarius 0) and Saturn (9 Aquarius 3), with only 3 minutes from an exact square aspect. This indicates a deep personal issue having to do with an authority figure and a vulnerability to exploitation which she has successfully been able to overcome.

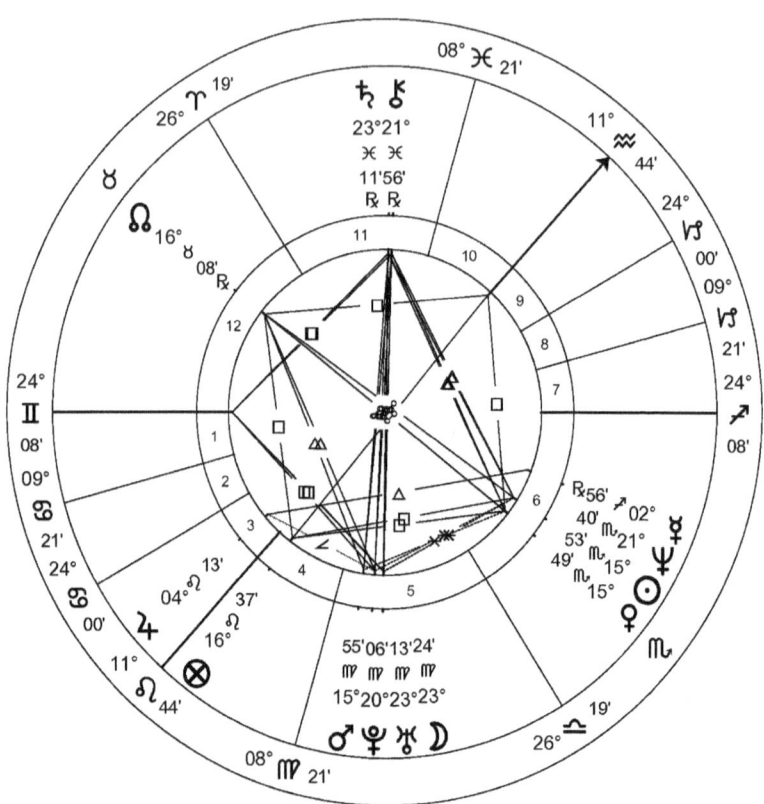

Natal Chart for Gordon Ramsay, 11/08/1966, 06:05 PM, Johnstone, Scotland

The next featured chart is that of famous British chef, TV personality and restaurateur, Gordon Ramsay.

You may remember him for being the host of the TV program on competitive cooking, "Hell's Kitchen." Gordon was named top chef in the UK and in 2000 was only the third person to have won three Catey Awards. He was appointed an OBE (Order of the British Empire) by Queen Elizabeth II for his services to the hospitality industry. He is a successful restaurateur having been awarded an impressive seventeen Michelin stars.

His Sun/Venus cazimi is six degrees from Neptune. After he was recognized as a top chef and restaurateur, he found his calling as a celebrity chef on TV programs. He has additional Category I, planetary conjunctions with his Moon in a partile conjunction to Uranus and conjunct Pluto.

Gordon's Mars is a little more than four degrees from Pluto. In his TV shows we can see his volatile nature displayed. There is also the opposition between the stern disciplined nature of Saturn to the perfection demands of the conjunction of Moon, Uranus and Pluto. Based on his reputation, he has been able to define a unique niche in the field of competitive cooking shows. He potentially has a Category II special conjunction with his Part of Fortune just five degrees from his IC.

The dynamics of his Moon in a partile conjunction to Uranus can be expressed through his critical outbursts during his TV shows. His anger and criticism are not simply for effect for TV viewers but part of his natural demeanor. With the stellium in his fifth house and cazimi in his sixth house he has been able to successfully merge his personality and creative cooking skills into the field of cooking as a form of business entertainment.

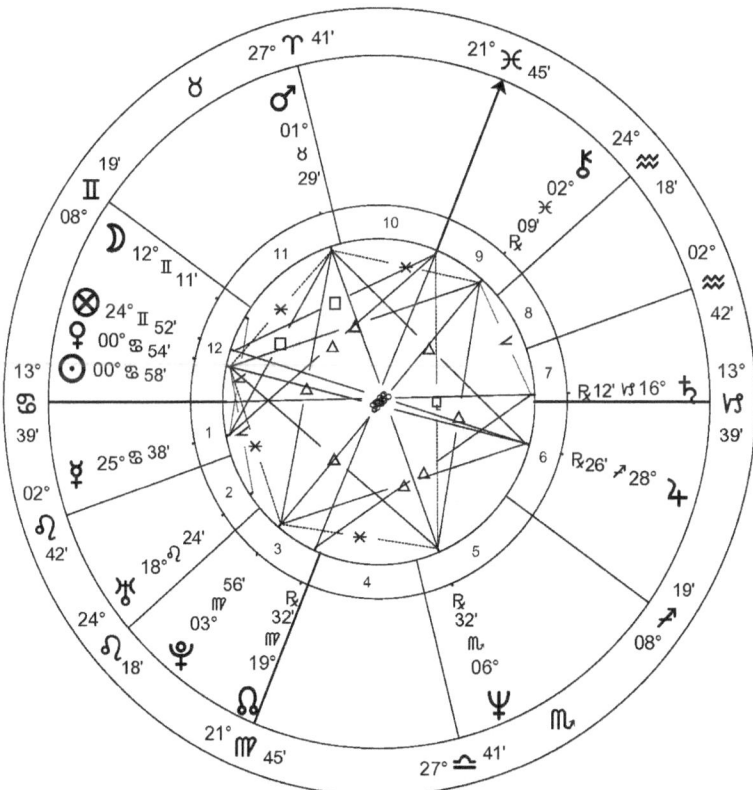

Natal Chart for Adam Schiff, 06/22/1960, 06:13 AM, Framingham, Massachusetts

Lucky Stars, Lucky Life   55

The next chart is not an entertainment celebrity but a politician, Adam Schiff. He graduated from Stanford University and Harvard Law School. He entered politics in 1996 and was elected to the California State Senate serving from 1996 to 2000. In 2000 he ran and defeated the incumbent for California's 27th Congressional district in the US House of Representatives. He announced his candidacy in January 2023, stating his intention to run for the US Senate in 2024 to succeed Diane Feinstein. Schiff was sucessful in winning the Senate seat in Novemeber 2024.

His Sun (0 Cancer 58) and Venus (0 Cancer 54) are separated from an exact conjunction by a mere 4 minutes having just entered the sign of Cancer in the twelfth house. With his Moon and Part of Fortune in Gemini and Mercury in his first house, he is very intelligent evidenced by his education. Prior to serving on the House Judiciary Committee, Adam Schiff was on the House Permanent Select Committee on Intelligence. As a former intelligence chairman, he was involved in twelfth house activities in closed door sessions having to do with classified intelligence matters. In addition to his Sun/Venus cazimi he has two Category II "lucky conjunctions" with his North Node conjunct his IC and Saturn on the Descendant that will serve him well. His Part of Fortune is six degrees from his Sun/Venus cazimi.

The next chart is that of Rick Warren, the former evangelical Christian pastor of Saddleback Church. The ruler of his Taurus Ascendant, Venus (8 Aquarius 02), conjunct his Sun (8 Aquarius 20) in his tenth house of public achievement and honors. With his cazimi situated in the highly elevated position in the tenth house he was destined to achieve accomplishments and honors. Aside from the Category I planetary conjunction of the Sun and Venus he has a second planetary conjunction of his Moon and Mars.

In 1980 Rick Warren, together with his wife, founded the Saddleback Church in Lake Forest, California. Its immense popularity and subsequent growth led it to become the largest mega church in Southern California. With the use of video conference technology and multiple campuses, his sermons in 2020 reached a weekly attendance of 28,000 parishioners. The Saddleback Church was ranked by Outreach Magazine as being among the top ten churches in the United States. He was the author of the best-selling book, "The Purpose Driven Life", which sold over thirty million copies.

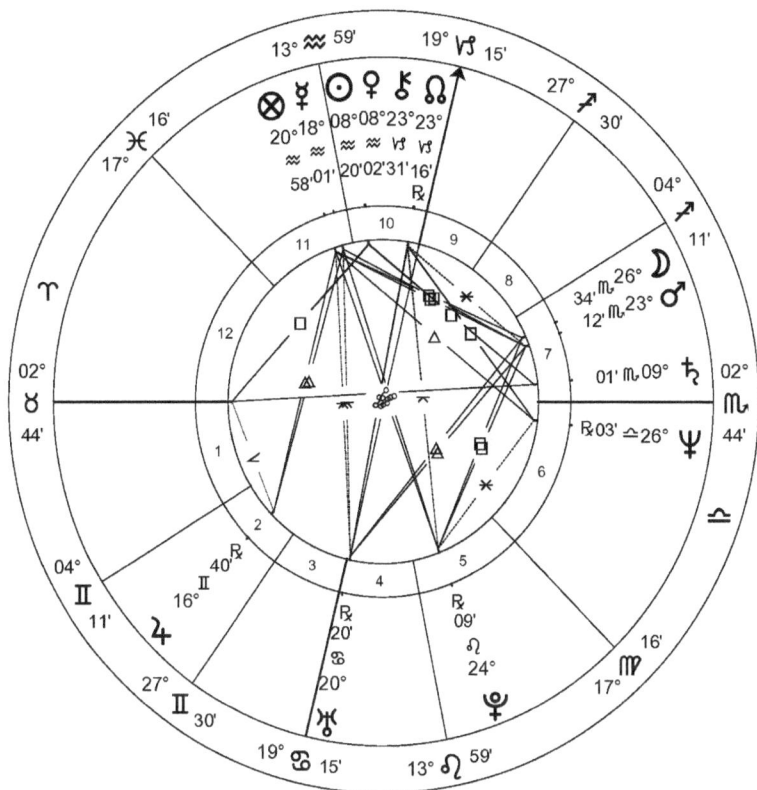

Natal Chart of Rick Warren, 01/28/1954, 11:01 AM, San Jose, California

His chart shows that in addition to his two Category I planetary conjunctions he has a couple of Category II special conjunctions. His Uranus is conjunct his IC, Mercury conjunct his Part of Fortune and his North Node just five degrees from his MC all positive indicators of success.

Rick Warren stepped down as head pastor in 2022. In February 2023 the Southern Baptist Church (SBC) expelled the Saddleback Church for theological differences, more specifically for having named three women pastors. After further review, the decision to expel the Saddleback Church from the SBC was reaffirmed in June 2023.

According to Sahl bin Bishr, a 9th century a Jew of Persian origin, the cazimi should apply to as much as one degree. If so, this would include Michele Ferrero, born in 1925 and deseased in 2015. He has a single

Lucky Stars, Lucky Life

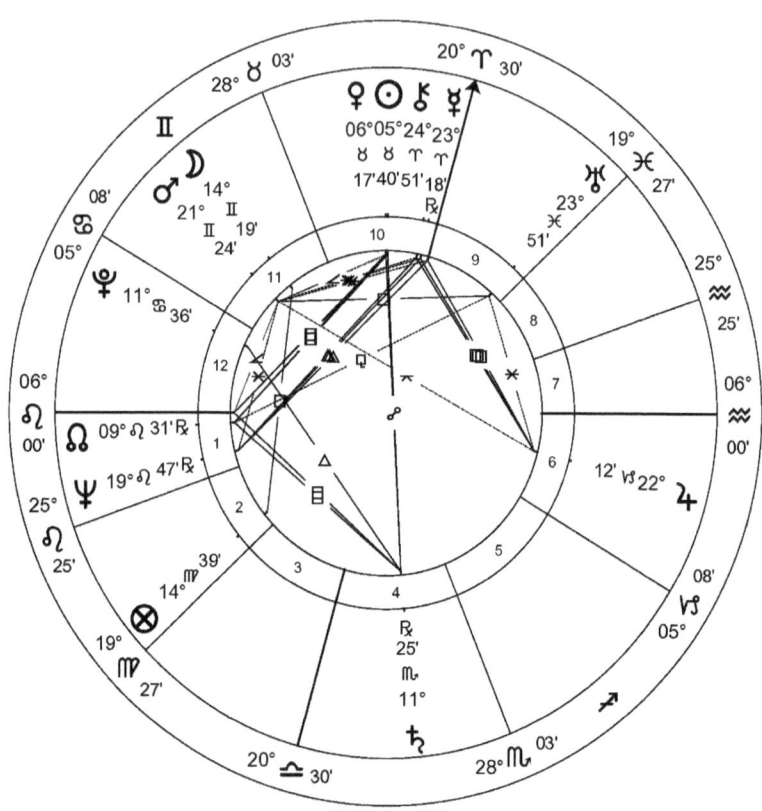

Natal Chart for Michele Ferrero, 04/26/1925, 11:30 AM, Cuneo, Italy

Category I "Lucky Star", the partile conjunction of Sun and Venus in his tenth house of achievement. He also is blessed with two Category II special conjunctions - Mercury conjunct his MC and his North Node conjunct his Ascendant. Like other successful individuals with a Sun/Venus cazimi he also has an opposition to the opposite hemisphere, sign and house.

Ferrero is not only an Italian billionaire, he is considered the richest man in Italy with an estimated net worth around $25 billion.

He built his family company, the Ferrero Group, into Europe's second largest confectionery company, and expanded the candy empire globally. Brands include the Ferrero Rocher chocolates, the Tic Tac brand, Butterfinger, as well as the chocolate and hazelnut spread, Nutella. After several prior acquisitions, Ferrero acquired in 2019 from Kellogg the "Famous Amos" brand of chocolate cookies founded by Wally Amos some

50 years ago. Wally Amos, a black entrepreneur, was also born with Sun partile Venus. He passed away in August 2024 in Honolulu, Hawaii.

Here is a more extensive list of those born during the cazimi of the Sun and Venus born during the twentieth century. If we extend the orb of the cazimi from its strict definition of 17 minutes, the number of famous individuals increases. *Delta minutes are minutes from an exact conjunction.*

Name	Date of Birth	Sun	Venus	* Delta Minutes
Emperor Hirohito	04/29/1901	8 Taurus 31	8 Taurus 06	25
Leona Helmsley	07/04/1921	12 Cancer 05	12 Cancer 14	9
Michele Ferrero	04/26/1925	5 Taurus 40	6 Taurus 18	38
Sathya Sai Baba	11/23/1926	29 Scorpio 58	0 Sagittarius 21	22
Wally Amos	07/01/1936	9 Cancer 12	9 Cancer 43	31
Ryan O'Neal	04/20/1941	0 Taurus 14	0 Taurus 35	21
Martin Scorsese	11/17/1942	24 Scorpio 24	24 Scorpio 21	3
Linda Evans	11/18/1942	25 Scorpio 29	25 Scorpio 58	29
Rick Warren	01/29/1952	8 Aquarius 03	8 Aquarius 20	17
Oprah Winfrey	01/29/1954	9 Aquarius 00	8 Aquarius 51	9
Adam Schiff	06/22/1960	0 Cancer 58	0 Cancer 54	4
Boris Johnson	06/19/1964	28 Gemini 27	28 Gemini 46	19
Gordon Ramsey	11/08/1966	15 Scorpio 53	15 Scorpio 49	4

As mentioned earlier, each of the individuals has an opposition aspect in their chart. An opposition bewtween two planets occurs roughly half the cases when there is a cazimi superior conjunction of the Sun and Venus. Here is a list of dates when a superior conjunction occurs during the second decade of this century.

Date	Degree/Sign	Opposition
March 26, 2021	6 Aries	No
October 22, 2022	29 Libra	Yes
June 4, 2024	14 Gemini	No
January 6, 2026	16 Capricorn	Yes
August 11, 2027	19 Leo	No
March 23, 2029	3 Aries	Yes

CHAPTER FIVE

JUPITER AND SATURN

While those born under a Sun and Venus partile conjunction or a cazimi are quite rare, there is a wider window of opportunity which can offer the development of a strong character and a good chance to become successful. It will come at a cost of hard work and sacrifice. I am referring to the Jupiter and Saturn conjunction.

The influence of Jupiter and Saturn can play an important role in an individual's life path. When these two planetary giants come together roughly every twenty years it is referred to as the Great Conjunction. Jupiter represents expansion, fame, growth, and optimism. Saturn is known by such keywords as the task master, discipline, hard work and often associated as the "father figure." So how can the two planets of such divergent qualities have such a strong influence in the chart? The combination often indicates a strong character and work ethic. It is not unusual with this combination to have an outgoing public presence. Individuals with this conjunction would likely have other Category I or Category II conjunctions to augment their chances for a successful life.

In Appendix II you may notice that there are several familiar names born during this conjunction. We can look back retrospectively at who has achieved fame and a name for themselves. We can also look forward to when it is one of the more favorable periods to be born that may indicate success.

This is in part because the two planets are slow moving, so the time frame when they are conjunct can be measured in months, rather than conjunctions involving faster moving personal planets (Mercury, Venus, and Mars) that can be measured in days or weeks.

Name	Category I Planetary Conjunctions	Category II Special Conjunctions
Alex Trebek	Sun/Mercury (P) Sun/Pluto	Venus/MC
Bernardo Bertolucci		Neptune/ASC (P) Sun/DSC (P)
Brian De Palma	Sun/Mars Mercury/Neptune (P) Venus/Pluto (P)	
Bruce Lee	Moon/Mercury	Sun/ASC
Dione Warwick		Moon/ASC Pluto/IC
Faye Dunaway	Sun/Mercury	Mars/IC
James Brolin	Mercury/Pluto (P)	NNode/ASC
Jessica Alba	Sun/Mercury	Moon/DSC Uranus/IC
Joan Baez	Sun/Mercury	
John Lennon	Sun/Moon	Sun/DSC
Martin Sheen	Sun/Moon	Mars/DSC PoF/ASC
Nick Nolte		Jupiter/ASC (P) Saturn/ASC Neptune/PoF
Pele	Mars/NNode (P)	
Placido Domingo		Mars/IC
Raquel Welch	Sun/Mercury Sun/Mars	
Richard Pryor	Venus/Mars (P)	
Ringo Starr	Moon/Mercury Mars/Pluto (P)	Neptune/DSC Venus/IC

Above I have listed the periods when Jupiter and Saturn were within three degrees of an exact conjunction.

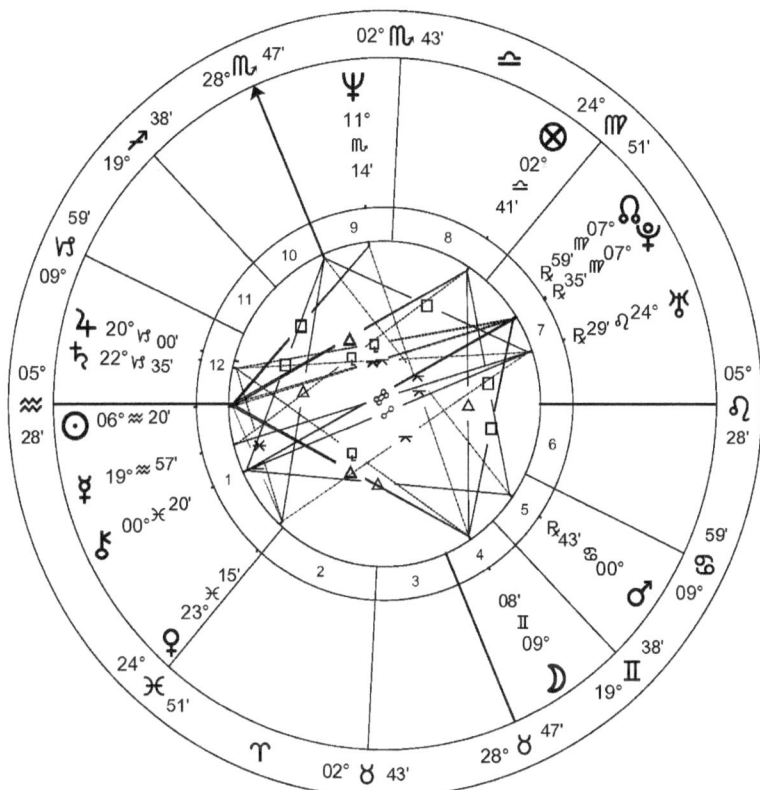

Natal Chart for Wayne Gretzsky, 01/26/1961, 07:45 AM, Brantford, Ontario, Canada

Most of the Jupiter and Saturn exact conjunctions occurred within a month but due to their retrograde motion the conjunctions covered a longer period.

The individuals noted above were born during July 1940 – March 1941 in the sign of Taurus. Their success in part shows that the Jupiter/Saturn conjunctions were augmented by other Category I planetary conjunctions and/or Category II special conjunctions. You may have noticed that two of the Beatles, John Lennon and Ringo Starr, were both born within three degrees of an exact conjunction of Jupiter and Saturn. In fact, John Lennon was born when Jupiter and Saturn were less than one degree apart.

Dr. Anthony Fauci, physician and immunologist serving as director of the National Institute of Allergy and Infectious Diseases from 1984 – 2022, was born under the Jupiter/Saturn conjunction on December

24, 1940 (time unknown). He acted as advisor to seven US presidents since Ronald Reagan. He served as the chief medical advisor to Donald Trump and one of the lead members of the White House COVID-19 Response Team. His strong convictions, in part from his Jupiter/Saturn conjunction, led to differences between himself and Donald Trump.

In February 1961 an exact conjunction of Jupiter and Saturn occurred in the earth sign of Capricorn. It was during this conjunction period that Wayne Gretzky, the Canadian former ice hockey player, was born. He has several Category I planetary conjunctions. In addition to the powerful and beneficial conjunction of Jupiter and Saturn and his Pluto partile conjunction to his North Node. The first degree of any sign is considered a critical degree. His Mars, the ruler of his Scorpio MC, is on 0 Cancer 43 of Cancer. For his Category II special conjunction, his Sun (6 Aquarius 21) lies on his Ascendant (5 Aquarius 29), giving the qualities of a double Aquarian. It gives a positive and confident impression to unleash his physical energy when demanded. All these factors contribute to his superstar status in the world of hockey.

The next chart belongs to a familiar name you may see on the television news is the political commentator, George Stephanopoulos. He served under the administration of Bill Clinton as the White House chief communications director and currently is the ABC News Chief Washington Correspondent. He was born on February 10, 1961. His Jupiter and Saturn are not only in a partile conjunction in Capricorn but are also conjunct his MC. This combination of Saturn as the ruler of Capricorn involves a successful career reporting about political affairs. He has his North Node conjunct Pluto and Mercury conjunct his Part of Fortune. This indicates George has the power to influence through the mass media. The Part of Fortune conjunct Mercury shows his success and career is congruent with his work in the field of communication.

The conjunction between Jupiter and Saturn conjunction that occurred at the turn of this century was between May 2000 – June 2000 in the sign of Taurus. The most recent conjunction of Jupiter and Saturn occurred December 19, 2020, at 0 Aquarius 2020. It will be interesting to see which individuals born during the conjunctions in 2000 and 2020 make a name for themselves.

The attributes of Jupiter and Saturn are associated with strong character and positive financial outlook. Taurus is the sign that garners respect for steadfastness, hard work, strong social and dependability. Taurus is ruled by the planet Venus, which brings qualities associated with beauty,

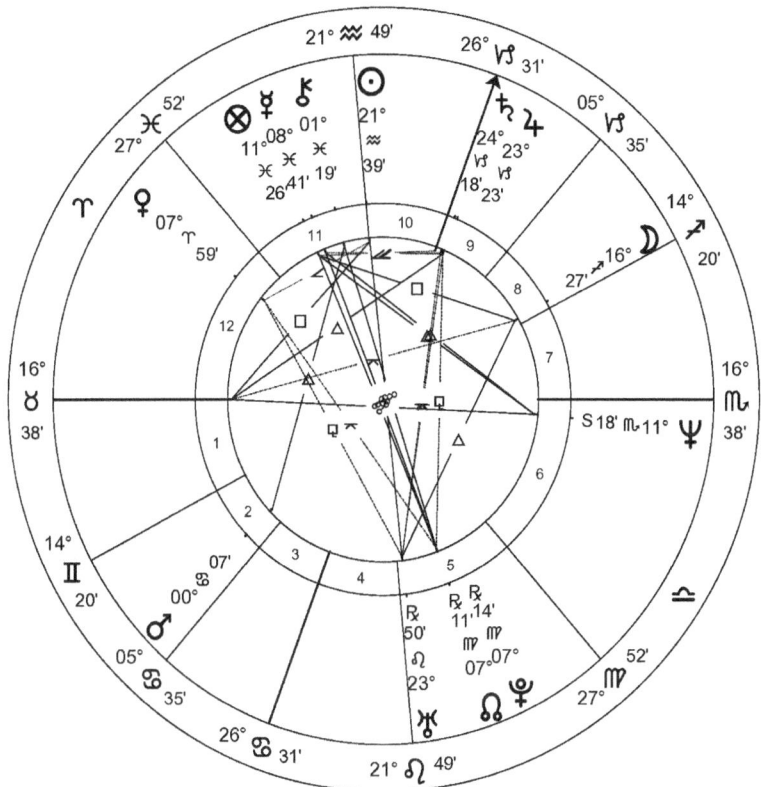

Natal Chart for George Stephanopoulos, 02/10/1961, 10:17 AM, Fall River, Massachusetts

arts, and entertainment. Capricorn is associated with strong organizational skills, perseverance and hard work. Aside from being born during this fortunate window in time these individuals often have additional Category I or Category II conjunctions to enhance their ability to attain fame.

The conjunction of Jupiter and Saturn also signifies strength of character, determination, and hard work. To see how this powerful combination is realized we should look at other planetary conjunctions in the chart. Most often it will be one of the personal planets (Sun, Moon, Mercury or Mars) or a personal planet working together with Uranus or Neptune.

Below I have listed the Category I and Category II conjunctions for some notable individuals born during the November 1980 – August 1981 Jupiter/Saturn conjunction. That conjunction occurred in the sign of Libra.

Name	Category I Planetary Conjunctions	Category II Special Conjunctions
Adriana Lima		Sun/DSC
Chris Evans		Uranus/ASC
Christina Aguilera	Sun/Neptune Mercury/Neptune Venus/Uranus	
Clara Morgane	Mercury/Mars (P)	NNode/MC (P)
Jake Gyllenhaal	Mercury/Neptune (P)	NNode/ASC
Jessica Alba	Sun/Mercury	Moon/DSC
Joseph Gordon-Levitt	Sun/Mercury (P)	Moon/NNode
Justin Timberlake	Moon/Neptune (P)	Jupiter/PoF Mars/DSC
Megan, Duchess of Sussex	Moon/Jupiter Moon/Saturn (P)	
Rami Malek		Moon/IC Pluto/PoF
Roger Federer		Sun/Mercury

Another individual, who exhibited power and authority having Sun in a partile conjunction to Saturn was George Wallace, four-time Governor of Alabama, who led the South's fight against racial integration in the 1960s. The combination of the Sun and Saturn tends to display life energies involving social interaction in roles of responsibility and leadership roles.

CHAPTER SIX

THE MOON'S NORTH NODE

In addition to planetary conjunctions, there are two kinds of non-planetary points that are not physically observable points in the sky. They are mathematically derived points. They are the Moon's Nodes and the Part of Fortune. The Part of Fortune will be covered in the next chapter. Any conjunctions of the planets to these points or to the axis points in the chart offer the gift of destiny and good fortune.

The Moon's Nodes and their importance in natal astrology is widely recognized by astrologers. Hindu astrologers refer to the North Node and South Node as Rahu and Ketu, respectively. In Western or tropical astrology, the North Node is referred to as the Dragon's Head and the South Node as the Dragon's Tail and they represent the most powerful influence in natal chart. They hold a deep spiritual and karmic significance affecting our destiny. The North Node indicates our life mission with qualities to be developed through conscious effort. The South Node refers to effort that was previously developed in past lifetime and therefore requires little effort to manifest. As the emphasis is to evolve assisted by what some consider destiny, we will focus our efforts just on the Moon's North Node.

Knowledge of the Moon's nodes has been known since ancient times. From an astronomical standpoint, the nodes of the Moon are related to solar and lunar eclipses. Each of the planets orbit the Sun and vary in their inclination of orbit to the ecliptic. The earth revolves around the Sun generally in zero inclination to the ecliptic compared to Pluto varies by as much as 17 degrees. If the Moon revolved around the earth at the same plane, or ecliptic, we would experience a lunar and solar eclipse every month. Instead, we experience a solar eclipse somewhere on our planet about once every eighteen months.

What are the Moon's nodes? They are points where the plane of the Moon's circuit intersects the plane of the Sun's ecliptic. When the Moon crosses going north of the ecliptic the crossing point is referred to as the North Node or Dragon's Head and when it goes south of the ecliptic is called the South Node, or Dragon's Tail. The two points are situated opposite each other in the natal chart. The nodes are especially significant during periods of eclipses.

US president Donald Trump not only has his Sun conjunct Uranus but conjunct his North Node. He is the only US president born during a lunar eclipse. In a lunar eclipse the Moon and Sun form an opposition aspect. His Sun and Uranus are in an opposition aspect to his Moon. That is responsible for his fervent emotional attacks against his detractors. All the while it appeals to supporters as a symbol of strength while feeding his ambitions.

The Moon's nodes move backward in all of the signs at a rate of 3 minutes per day or about 19 degrees per year. The cycle of the Moon's nodes is every 18.6 years. The cosmic impact of the Moon's nodes upon lunar and solar eclipses can have a powerful effect upon an individual as well as upon the destiny of nations has been covered in astrology books.

Planets conjunct the North Node signify qualities to be developed or nurtured compared to planets conjunct the South Node are qualities previously developed. The North and South Node are in the opposite hemisphere, sign, and house. For example, if the North Node is at 13 Aries, the South Node would be situated at 13 Libra. When the North Node is situated on any of the angles, (the Ascendant/MC/Descendant/IC) this strongly indicates that the individual is particularly fateful or predestined.

You may want to observe when the Moon's nodes conjunct or transit the planets in your chart. Like planetary conjunctions, we have shown how the placement of the North and South Node affect individuals, especially when they are conjunct the Sun, Moon, or at the cusp of the tenth house, or Midheaven. A planet or Part of Fortune conjunction with the North Node adds special qualities of the planet as part of their spiritual development. When we find planets that are conjunct to the North Node one should check what sign and house it is located.

You will find that many of the people named in Appendix II with planets conjunct to their North Node are very successful. It is due in part by other "Lucky Stars" and non-planetary conjunctions or planets that are situated on the four axis points. This makes the meanings of planets conjunct the North Node difficult to attribute to a single feature that has contributed to their success. It also demonstrates that achieving fame and fortune is often a combination of planetary features. Despite this, I have briefly shared some insights into qualities where the North Node is conjoined with a planet or axis point to emphasize the individual's special task in this life.

Most people who attained considerable achievement and success in their life have certain qualities represented by planetary conjunctions and non-planetary influences. Good fortune is linked to planets conjunct their Part of Fortune and their North Node. Here are some ideas to consider when is planet is conjunct the North Node.

North Node/Ascendant – This would depend on if it was located in the 1st house or 12th. If in the 12th house the North Node would act like the rising planet at dawn. A destiny that will propel a lifetime of personal and professional elevation.

North Node/Sun - There is considerable luck, and privilege, self-recognition and material wealth. It may be accompanied by a high degree of self-importance and strong ego. An example of great fortune can be seen in the chart of Bernard Marcus, founder of Home Depot. He was born May 12, 1929 (birth time unknown), he has his North Node (21 Taurus 18) conjunct his Sun (21 Taurus 25), conjunct Jupiter (22 Taurus 47).

North Node/Moon – The Moon rules our emotions and strong female qualities. Those with this feature have a unique ability to identify with the public and what they seek. It brings to bear the deep dependency or emotional connection upon one's mother, the need for the security of home and family. The emotions are heightened and there is an increase in psychic sensitivity. These individuals may be able to garner public support and do well in public eye. They may find the entertainment industry or even politics appealing.

North Node/Mercury – Your intellect and ability to express yourself will assist you in achieving your success. You have an intellect that is adaptable and strong powers of the intellect. You are destined to be naturally intellectually gifted and a visionary. An example is Wernher von Braun, the former German Nazi and German rocket scientist.

Following WWII he was moved to the US under the highly secret Operation Paperclip. He then worked on the US ballistic missile technology and became the first director at NASA

North Node/Venus - Your sense of values and importance of love and affection will transform you. Often charming and loving, you make good peacemakers, referees, judges, and diplomats to soothe differences. This combination appeals to the finer senses of art and music.

North Node/Mars – People with this nodal combination possess a lot of energy to achieve their goals. This may be someone that is attracted to sports and is athletic. It does not necessarily involve brute physical strength but the ability to compete and the endurance to excel in their field. They are driven by their personal drive to achieve their destiny. Examples of those with Mars conjunct their North Node include Lance Armstrong, Mark Wahlberg, and Pele.

One of the most decorated Olympians in 2024 was the famed American gymnast, Simon Biles. She has three Category I planetary conjunctions: Sun conjunct Mercury, Sun conjunct Venus and Mars conjunct her North Node.

North Node/Jupiter – Your destiny will be enhanced by Jupiter qualities of generosity, abundance and altruism. Jupiter is also associated with philosophy in the search of gaining wisdom.

North Node/Saturn – Your success will be marked by your strength of character. Saturn is thought of as the teacher to instill self-reliance, patience, and responsibility.

North Node/Uranus - Uranus tries to rebel or eliminate what is outworn and unnecessary. Uranus is future oriented and brings with it new ideas. This is sometimes through new inventions and advances in technology. Your destiny is through discarding the old and bringing forth new approaches and fresh ideas. Some appeal to seek change upon the social and political order. They often have longer term consequences to be considered. There seems to be a penchant for those with Uranus conjunct the North Node to be quite vocal and revolutionary in spreading their message.

Those who achieve success with Uranus conjunct the North Node can be considered unique and out of the box as these individuals are one of a kind. They are radical and even revolutionary, carried away with their own ideas. Their boldness can take them so far until they must face the consequences of their actions.

One of our most controversial US generals was General Armstrong Custer. He was born on December 5, 1839 (time unknown). He has two Category I planetary conjunctions. His Sun is in a partile conjunction to his Saturn and Uranus is conjunct to his North Node. He is portrayed as an American hero during the Battle of the Bighorn, known as Custer's Last Stand, when he died along with 200 of his men.

There is a little-known side of General Custer. Although he was known for his fearlessness and aggressiveness, critics claim he was brash, ostentatious, and a publicity hound. He was known for his pranks while attending West Point and graduated last in his class. Prior to graduating from West Point he was court martialed twice.

Custer struggled in the classroom. It was his leadership qualities displayed by his bold and brash actions that enabled him to be eventually promoted to the rank of brigadier general at the age of twenty-three.

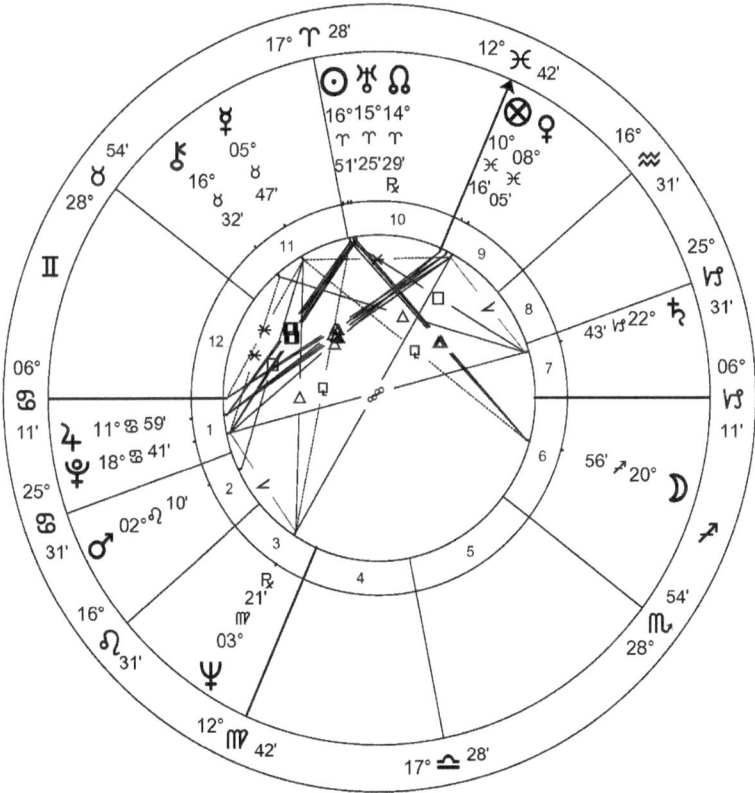

Natal Chart for Daniel Ellsberg, 04/07/1931, 09:47 AM, Chicago, Illinois

Another example is Daniel Ellsberg who was a controversial figure in 1971. He was an American political and military analyst. He rose to prominence with the release of what is known as the Pentagon Papers, a highly classified study relating to America's involvement and expansion of the Vietnam War. It also served as the beginning of the turning point in the presidency of Richard Nixon.

The release of the "Pentagon Papers" led to the break-in of Daniel Ellsberg's psychiatrist's office. This was followed by the break-in of the Democratic National Committee headquarters, leading to the Watergate scandal and the eventual downfall of then President Richard Nixon. Daniel Ellsberg had been employed by the think tank, the Rand Corporation. In 1973 he was charged under the Espionage Act of 1917 along with other charges of espionage, theft of government property, and conspiracy carrying a maximum sentence of 115 years. These charges against him were later dismissed.

Daniel Ellsberg has his Sun, Uranus and North Node all within three degrees of each other. He has Category II special conjunctions of Venus conjunct his Part of Fortune and Part of Fortune conjunct his MC. One might wonder if the dismissal of the charges against him were in part due to the fortunate luck of his Part of Fortune conjunct his MC. He has a T-Cross with the opposition of Saturn (government) to Pluto both in a square aspect to his Sun and Uranus. He passed away in June 2023.

Another notable historical figure with Uranus conjunct his North Node is Ayatollah Khomeini, the founder of the Islamic Republic of Iran, born on May 17, 1900 (birth time unknown).

He was born when Jupiter (7 Sagittarius 19), North Node (10 Sagittarius 58) and Uranus (11 Sagittarius 06) were conjunct each other. If you recall, Sagittarius is associated with religion. He brought about his personal conservative, structured, disciplined religious approach to the rest of his country, Iran. If we look at his chart there is a cardinal T-Cross with Jupiter, North Node and Uranus square both to Saturn and Pluto. Saturn (22 Capricorn 42) is in opposition to Pluto (18 Cancer 42).

Those familiar with history, may remember him as the leader of the Iranian Revolution of 1979 and the overthrow of the Shah of Iran, Mohammad Reza Pahlavi. Amid the Iranian Revolution there was the international crisis beginning in November 1979 when militant Iranian college students supporting the Iranian Revolution seized 53 American diplomats and citizens as hostages and held them for 444 days before they were released.

Ayatollah Khomeini was the highest ranking political and religious leader of the Islamic Republic until he died in 1989.

Throughout my research, I found that individuals having a conjunction to Uranus or Pluto to their Part of Fortune or the North Node possess unique personality traits. It should not go unnoticed that Uranus appears prominently in the charts of US presidents. The first four of our twenty first century presidents were born with Uranus conjunct their North Node. I am referring to Bill Clinton, George W. Bush, Barack Obama and Donald Trump. The close presidential contenders, despite their gallant efforts, were no match against this powerful karmic connection. Each of the four twenty first century presidents were born to lead. They either had Leo as their Rising Sign (George W. Bush, Donald Trump) or born in the sign of Leo (Bill Clinton, Barak Obama). Leos have a love for the attention of the center stage. Leo is represented symbolically by the lion, the king of the jungle. This sign is associated with a flair for the dramatic and an affinity for leadership.

There have been five presidential elections in which the winning candidate lost the popular vote. The closest was when Al Gore conceded his defeat to George W. Bush. The voting count was so controversial that it led to the involvement of the US Supreme Court. Al Gore had lost by less than 600 popular votes in the State of Florida. The electoral votes went in favor of George W. Bush in the US presidential election of 2000. Al Gore had Leo Rising in his chart, but did not have Uranus conjunct his North Node. Hillary Clinton in her presidential bid in 2016 had neither Leo Ascendant, Sun in Leo or Uranus conjunct her North Node. Such is the outcome of destiny.

North Node/Neptune – Neptune is the planet of hopes, wishes and desires. You can achieve your highest good through sensitivity, inspiration and compassion. It is associated with delusion and illusion. Multiple planetary conjunctions involving the Sun, Uranus and the North Node can be associated with a leader of a movement or cult.

Cults, often headed by a charismatic leader, are not limited to the United States. Pseudo religious groups, cults, exist worldwide and even in the most technologically advanced countries. A cult leader and convicted con man, not familiar to most Americans is that of a Frenchman, named Joseph di Mambro. He founded and led the Order of the Solar Temple. In October 1994 he convinced over 50 cult members to die in an act of mass suicide/murder.

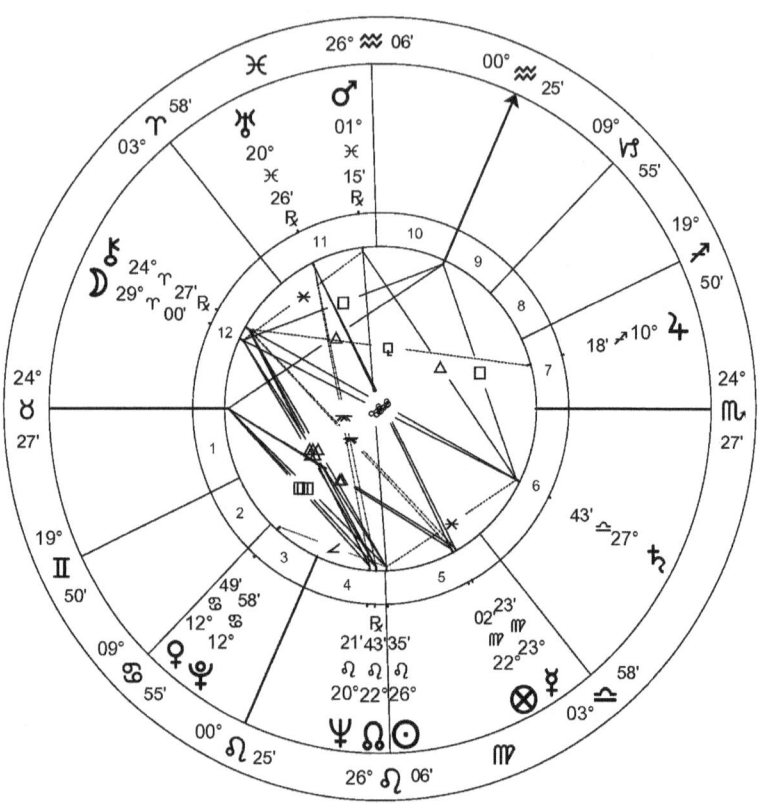

Natal Chart for Joseph di Mambro, 08/19/1924, 11:00 PM, Pont-St.-Espirit, France

His Category I planetary conjunctions include his Sun conjunct his North Node, Neptune conjunct his North Node, and Venus in a partile conjunction to Pluto.

His Category II special conjunction has Mercury conjunct his Part of Fortune with fanatical tenacity.

The ability of cult leaders to lure their supporters (with fanatical tenacity) to their own vision is legendary. Even in their defeat they continue to hold a visionary goal. The noted astrologer, Noel Tyl, in his book "*Aspects and Houses in Analysis,*" mentions how Adolph Hitler through self-delusion, driven by ambition, was able to propel a mighty nation towards pursuit of his vision. It is a miracle of practical achievement.

Unfortunately, cult leaders like Jim Jones, Marshall Applewhite, and Joseph di Mambro, when faced with defeat bring their followers down with them. There are modern day political leaders (such as Hitler) that have been able to convince their followers, often through the mass media and propaganda, to their causes. When faced with failure, they are willing to sacrifice their army of "soldiers" and ardent supporters. They end up destroying the lives of millions of innocent people and their country as well. When they fail, they often blame others for their own shortcomings.

North Node/Pluto – Here the life path or life journey of an individual can be a meaningful one.

Individuals with a Pluto/North Node possess an incredible amount of willpower and determination. These individuals lead a distinguished though a fateful life.

North Node/MC –Such an individual may find recognition and success as their destiny.

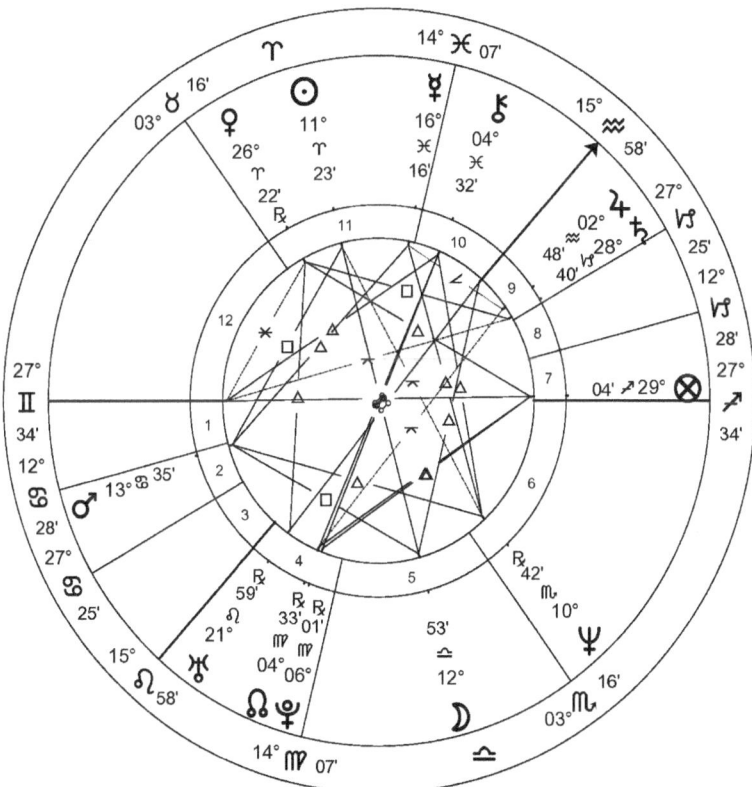

Natal Chart for Susan Boyle, 04/01/1961, 09:50 AM, Bangour Village Hospital, Scotland

Sometimes a talented individual just needs the right opportunity or a lucky break before they are discovered and propelled into a life of fame and wealth. This has spawned a number of national talents shows and open mic shows at comedy clubs to get exposure. The performing arts such as acting, singing, dancing, magic, and various other genres are encouraged to audition awaiting the opportunity to be discovered. Such is the case with Susan Boyle.

Looking at the chart of Susan Boyle she has no planetary conjunctions other than Pluto conjunct her North Node just 8 minutes from an exact conjunction. She was born during a Full Moon, with her Sun at 11 Aries 24 is in opposition to her Moon at 12 Libra 53. Consequently, her Part of Fortune is conjunct her Descendant.

This Scottish amateur singer came to public attention at the age of forty-eight, when she appeared in April 2009 as a contestant of Britain's Got Talent. It was her first public appearance before a group larger than her parish church. Despite the audience's initial cynicism about her age, un-groomed appearance and weight, her vocal performance was outstanding. She sang "I Dreamed a Dream" from Les Miserables. Her performance transformed her into an international phenomenon. She has since released several albums and performances. Susan even has the distinction of having performed before Queen Elizabeth II and the Pope.

On the next page is a partial list of individuals born under the powerful influence of Pluto conjunct their North Node.

Name	Rodden Rating	Category I Planetary Conjunctions	Category II Special Conjunctions
Angela Davis	AA	Mars/Uranus	
Barry Goldwater	DD	Sun/Uranus Merc/Uranus(P)	
Billie Jean King	AA	Moon/Neptune	Saturn/PoF
Dennis Rodman	AA		Jupiter/PoF Neptune/MC
Fidel Castro	DD	Sun/Neptune	Mars/PoF
George Clooney	AA	Moon/Saturn Sun/Mercury	
George Stephanopoulos	AA	Jupiter/Saturn (P)	Mercury/PoF Jupiter/Sat/MC
Joe Frazier	DD	Mars/Uranus (P)	Uranus/PoF
John Denver	AA	Mars/Uranus (P)	
Joseph McCarthy	AA		PoF/MC Mars/DSC Uranus/MC
Justin Bieber	B	Mercury/Mars Neptune/Uranus	Pluto/ASC
Keith Richards	A	Mars/Uranus	Moon/MC PoF/IC
Randy Newman	A		Saturn/PoF
Susan Boyle	AA		PoF/DSC
Victor Borge	AA	Sun/Uranus Mercury/Uranus	Venus/MC Neptune/PoF
Wayne Gretzky	AA	Jupiter/Saturn	Sun/ASC
George Adamski	A	Neptune/NNode Neptune/Pluto	
Shohei Otani	X	Moon/Mars (P) Uranus/Neptune	

CHAPTER SEVEN

THE PART OF FORTUNE

What is the Part of Fortune? It is not a planetary body but a mathematical construct. Although its actual origin is obscure, early Arabic astronomers produced a sophisticated body of astronomical work including what we know as the Arabian Parts. The Part of Fortune is one of the most used Arabian parts in astrology. Its glyph, or symbol, is a cross within a circle, the circle representing the Earth.

The principal bodies involved in the Part of Fortune are the Ascendant, Sun and the Moon. Some might call it destiny. It shows the close relation between the Sun, individuality and the instinctive nature of the Moon. It is a sensitive point in the chart that can generate great opportunities for material success.

Most astrological charts will typically display the Moon's Nodes but may not include the Part of Fortune. The Part of Fortune is the point on the natal chart associated with worldly success. If you know your time of birth, your Ascendant and your Moon, the Part of Fortune can be calculated.

There are two ways to compute your Part of Fortune, depending on whether you were born at night or during the day. If your Sun is above the horizon, the Ascendant-Descendant axis, you were born during the day. If you were born at night, the Sun would be below the Ascendant-Descendant axis.

ASCENDANT + MOON − SUN (DAY BIRTH)
Example:
Ascendant: 21 Gemini 22.
Sun: 0 Gemini 45.
Moon: 20 Leo 28.
The calculation is as follows: Degree/Sign/Minute.
Ascendant: 21 Gemini 22 = 21 3 22 (3 = Gemini, the third sign of the zodiac).
Moon: 20 Leo 28 = 20 5 28 (5 = Leo, the fifth sign of the zodiac).
When added: 41 8 50.
Minus the Sun: 0 3 45 (3 = Gemini, the third sign of the zodiac).
Equals: 41 5 05.
11 6 05: Here we reduce 41 by 30 and increase the sign.
The converted result is: 11 Virgo 5.

ASCENDANT + SUN − MOON (NIGHT BIRTH)
Example:
Ascendant: 16 Gemini 40.
Sun: 3 Sagittarius 29.
Moon: 2 Gemini 56.
The calculation is as follows: Degree/Sign/Minute.
Ascendant: 16 Gemini 40 = 16 3 40 (3 = Gemini, the third sign of the zodiac).
Sun: 3 Sagittarius 29 = 3 9 29 (9 = Sagittarius, the ninth sign of the zodiac).
When added: 19 12 69.
Minus the Moon: 2 3 56 (3 = Gemini, the third sign of the zodiac).
Equals: 17 9 13.
The converted result is: 17 Sagittarius 13.

The Part of Fortune is based on the same distance by longitude from the Ascendant as the Moon lies from the Sun. When the Sun and Moon are exactly conjunct each other, at the New Moon, the Part of Fortune would be located at the Ascendant. Consequently, when the Sun and Moon are exactly opposite each, or born exactly during a Full Moon, the Part of Fortune would be conjunct the Descendant. By the way, the example calculation above (evening birth), is that of Ricardo Montalban.

Ricardo Montalban, a Mexican and American television and film actor, was born on 6:10 pm on November 25, 1920, in Mexico City. Like many of my generation, I enjoyed the fantasy TV drama (1977 to

1984), *Fantasy Island*, starring Mr. Roark, portrayed by Ricardo Montalban. He was a double Gemini. His Moon is 2 Gemini 56 and is in his twelfth house at 2 Gemini 56 with his Ascendant is at 16 Gemini 40. He was born during a Full Moon and as such, his Part of Fortune is at 17 Sagittarius 12 rests on his Descendant.

His chart shows no planetary conjunctions, but astrologers will note that the Sun/Moon opposition are both square to his Uranus (1 Pisces 51) and his MC forming a T-Cross. The other notable feature is that his Uranus is less than four degrees from his MC.

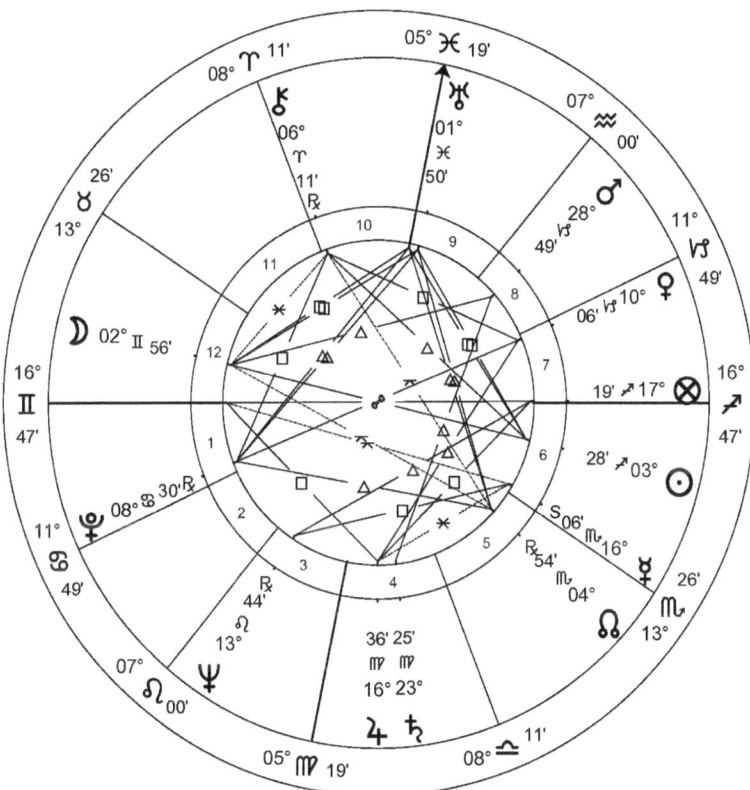

Natal Chart for Ricardo Montalban, 11/25/1920, 06:10 PM, Mexico City, Mexico

While there are certainly advantages of having multiple Category I and Category II conjunctions, there are those who do not have any planetary conjunctions. Yet it can take only a single key feature in their chart to lead to a life of fame and good fortune.

The following chart is that of famed actress of stage and screen, director, producer, screenwriter, author of three memoirs, and now social media star, Diane Keaton.

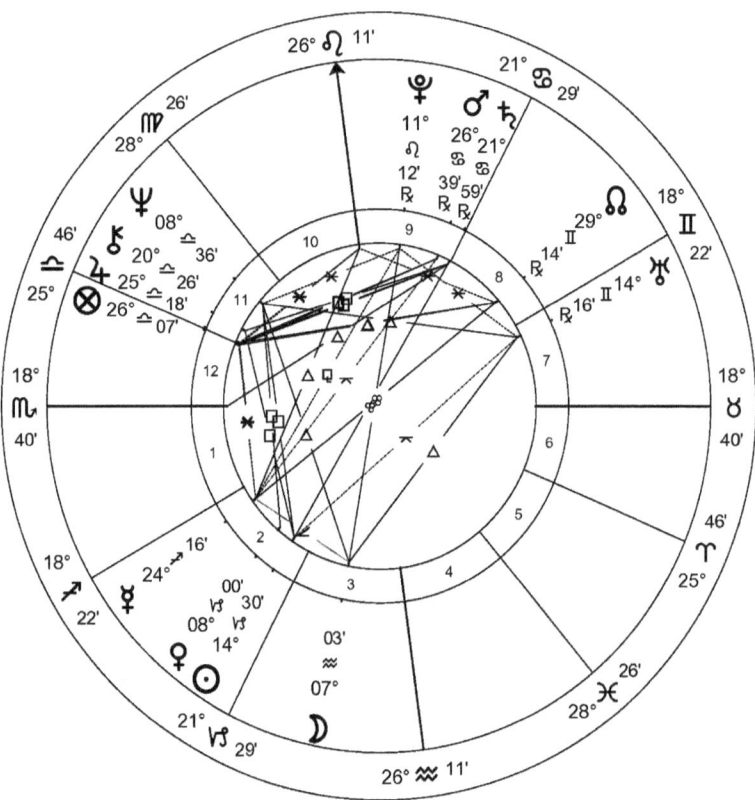

Natal Chart for Diane Keaton, 11/05/1946, 02:49 AM, Los Angeles, California

The only "Lucky Star" she has is Jupiter (25 Libra 19) in an almost perfect partile conjunction to her Part of Fortune (26 Libra 07), separated by just 12 minutes. Needless to say, she has been blessed by Jupiter, the planet of expansion and abundance and the good fortune of a successful acting career and popularity. There is a strong trine aspect between her Moon in Aquarius and Neptune in Libra. The tightest planetary aspect is Neptune 37 in Libra, a square aspect to Venus at 8 Capricorn 01, only 24 minutes to a square aspect. Both planetary combinations refer to her natural beauty and the movie industry.

Her good fortune has provided her with financial security to explore new realms.

Continuing with the "Lucky Star" theme, we will now only look at planets that are conjunct the Part of Fortune.

Part of Fortune to the Sun or Moon – As it involves the basic elements of the Part of Fortune, it indicates a unification of one's personality and individuality to achieve personal growth and fortune.

Part of Fortune/Mercury – You have an ability to achieve happiness through your expression of your thoughts and ideas. An ideal career could be involvement in publicity, advertising, news commentator, or involvement in social media.

Part of Fortune/Venus – Happiness associated with harmony and appreciation of artistic qualities.

Part of Fortune/Mars – Mars energy enables one to achieve good fortune.

Part of Fortune/Jupiter – A very lucky combination deserving of a wonderful and memorable life. A life of positive attitude, good fortune and abundance through a long and successful career.

Part of Fortune/Saturn – Happiness and opportunity through hard work.

Part of Fortune/Uranus - This combination is likely to achieve personal success through your unique thoughts and actions. You are likely to find your passion or goal in life in a very independent way and pursue unconventional interests.

Part of Fortune/Neptune – These individuals have a good deal of intuitive awareness, creativity and spiritual awareness. You may find satisfaction working for a social cause or involved in a religious organization.

Part of Fortune/Pluto – Good fortune often achieved through peak performance or mastership.

Part of Fortune/Ascendant –With the Part of Fortune on your Ascendant you can integrate your individuality and personality in achieving your goals through positive energy and emotional commitment.

Part of Fortune/MC: Those fortunate to have a planet conjunct their Ascendant or MC appear to live a happier, healthier and fulfilling life.

CHAPTER EIGHT

CONCLUSION

As the Sun and Moon are the major significators of one's personality and individuality, I have listed the zodiacal sign of the planet conjunct the Sun and the Moon in Appendix II. The most commonly occurring conjunction is Sun conjunct Mercury.

In Appendix II you will find the names that you may or may not be familiar with. If you are blessed to be born under a "Lucky Star", you should nurture and take advantage of it. It is extremely helpful if you have special conjunctions in addition to any planetary conjunction you may have. After I tell individuals of the qualities of their "Lucky Star", they tell me that it is something that they resonate with it or that "they always thought so" or words to that effect.

Most of the individuals listed in the Appendix II rarely achieved their success overnight. They have honed their skills and talents, seeking opportunities to achieve further recognition and success. Real happiness brings joy and satisfaction through a sense of purpose and meaning to life. Often those who have achieved the rewards of a "Lucky Life" lend their time and celebrity status to support any number of humanitarian, environmental or various charities/causes.

The list of names in Appendix II may include individuals you do not recognize. These people have a considerable net worth or have been recognized for their achievement in their field. Accurate birth data for many very wealthy and successful individuals is not always available. Many prefer to live their lives privately without being under the scrutiny of the press. On the other hand, there are celebrities that thrive on publicity and social media.

The column RR in the Appendix stands for Rodden rating. The highest rating is AA based on the birth certificate. The rating decreases as the accuracy of the time of birth or reliability declines to a rating of X if we only know the date of birth but are names of individuals that the reader might be curious about. I also abbreviated names of planets, the North Node and the Part of Fortune due to space limitations. Conjunctions that are just outside the limits I have set are identified by a bracket around the conjunction. I felt these aspects were important or significant enough to be noted.

I did not include conjunctions with asteroids which have a unique psychological quality. In personal consultations, astrologers may take into consideration the influence and interpretation of the major asteroids, Sabian symbols and fixed stars. In short, I wanted to keep the methodology as basic and simple as possible.

In closing, I hope that you have enjoyed this introductory exploration into the world of astrology and specifically conjunctions. If you enjoyed reading this book and the concept of "Lucky Stars, Lucky Life", the power of planetary and special conjunctions, please recommend it to others.

APPENDIX I

BIRTH DATA BY CHAPTER

CHAPTER ONE
- Katy Perry, October 25, 1984, 07:58am, Santa Barbara, California, RR: AA
- Rhonda Byrne, March 21, 1951, Melbourne, Australia, RR: X
- Lucky Luciano, November 24, 1897, 12:00pm, Lercara Friddi, Italy, RR: AA

CHAPTER TWO
- Imelda Marcos, July 02, 1929, 05:30am, Manila, Phillipines, RR: AA
- Jim Jones, May 13, 1931, 10:00pm, Lynn, Indiana, RR: AA

CHAPTER THREE
- Ted Kaczynski, May 22, 1942, 06:45am, Chicago, Illinois, RR: AA
- Donald Trump, June 14, 1946, 10:54am, Queens, New York, RR: AA

CHAPTER FOUR
- Leone Helmsley, July 04, 1920, 06:00am, Marbletown, New York, RR: AA
- Martin Scorsese, November 17, 1942, 12:24am, Flushing, New York. RR: AA
- Oprah Winfrey, January 29, 1954, 04:30am, Kosciusko, Mississippi, RR: A
- Gordon Ramsay, November 08, 1966, 06:05pm, Johnstone, Scotland, RR: AA
- Adam Schiff, June 22, 1960, 06:13am, Framingham, Massachusetts, RR: AA
- Rick Warren, January 28, 1954, 11:01am, San Jose, California, RR: AA
- Michele Ferrero, April 26, 1925, 11:30am, Cuneo, Italy, RR: AA

CHAPTER FIVE
- Wayne Gretzsky, January 26, 1961, 07:45am, Brantford, Ontario, Canada, RR: AA
- George Stephanopoulos, February 10, 1961, 10:17am, Fall River, Massachusetts, RR: AA

CHAPTER SIX
- Daniel Ellsberg, April 07, 1931, 09:47am, Chicago, Illinois, RR: AA
- Joseph di Mambro, August 19, 1924, 11:00pm, Pont-St.-Espirit, France, RR: AA
- Susan Boyle, April 01, 1961, 09:50am, Bangour Village Hospital, Scotland, RR: AA

CHAPTER SEVEN
- Ricardo Montalban, November 25, 1920, 06:10pm, Mexico City, Mexico, RR: AA
- Diane Keaton, November 05, 1946, 02:49am, Los Angeles, California, RR: AA

APPENDIX II

PLANETARY AND SPECIAL CONJUNCTIONS

Sun and Moon	RR	Name	Category I Planetary Conjunctions	Category II Special Conjunctions
Sun/Moon Aquarius	AA	Arsenio Hall	Jupiter/Pluto (P)	Venus/IC NNode/ASC (P)
Sun/Moon Aquarius	A	Beatrix of the Netherlands	Sun/Venus (P) Moon/Jupiter Venus/Jupiter Mars/Saturn (P)	
Sun/Moon Aries	AA	Brigette Macron	Sun/Venus (P) Moon/Venus Saturn/Neptune	Jupiter/MC
Sun/Moon Pisces	AA	Cindy Crawford	Mercury/Mars Mars/Saturn (P) Uran/Pluto (P)	
Sun/Moon (P) Aquarius	AA	Clint Black	Sun/Mercury Moon/Merc (P) Merc/Venus (P) Merc/Jupiter Venus/Jup (P) Mars/Saturn	PoF/ASC (P) (Pluto/PoF)
Sun/Moon Cancer	AA	Harrison Ford		PoF/ASC Mercury/MC
Sun/Moon Taurus	A	Jane Roberts	Sun/NNode Moon/NNode Jup/NNode (P)	PoF/ASC PoF/Saturn Saturn/PoF
Sun/Moon Scorpio	AA	Jenifer (Bartoli)	Sun/Venus Sun/Moon/ Mercury/Jupiter Sun/Jupiter (P) Saturn/Pluto (P)	
Sun/Moon (P) Sagittarius	AA	Lucky Luciano	Sun/Mars (P) Sun/Saturn (P) Sun/Uranus Moon/Sat (P) Mars/Saturn Mars/Uranus	Sun/Moon/ Saturn/MC PoF/ASC

Sun and Moon	RR	Name	Category I Planetary Conjunctions	Category II Special Conjunctions
Sun/Moon Aries	AA	Marlon Brando		Uranus/IC PoF/ASC
Sun/Moon Taurus	AA	Marshall Applewhite	Jupiter/Pluto	PoF/ASC
Sun/Moon Leo	AA	Martin Sheen	Jup/Saturn (P)	PoF/ASC Mars/DSC
Sun/Moon Sun/Sagittarius Moon/Scorpio	AA	Miley Cyrus	Venus/Uranus Uranus/Nept/ Moon/Merc (P) Moon/Merc/ Pluto	Sun/Moon/ Mercury/DSC
Sun/Moon Aquarius	AA	Princess Stephanie of Monaco	Mercury/Venus Uranus/Pluto	Jupiter/MC PoF/ASC
Sun/Moon (P) Gemini	A	Salman Rushdie	Sun/Uranus Moon/Uranus	Mercury/IC PoF/ASC
Sun/Moon Cancer	AA	William, Prince of Wales		Sun/DSC Jupiter/MC Neptune/ASC

Sun	RR	Name	Category I Planetary Conjunctions	Category II Special Conjunctions
Sun/Mercury (P) Cancer	A	Alex Trebek	Sun/Pluto Jup/Saturn(P)	Venus/MC
Sun/Mercury Sagittarius	A	Billy Idol	Mars/Neptune Jupiter/Pluto	Saturn/PoF Uranus/IC
Sun/Mercury Sagittarius	X	Chelsea Manning	Sun/Saturn Sun/Uranus Merc/Saturn Moon/Mars (P) Moon/Pluto	
Sun/Mercury Sagittarius	AA	Chris Evert	Moon/Saturn Moon/Venus Venus/Saturn Jupiter/Uranus	Pluto/MC NNode/PoF
Sun/Mercury Capricorn	AA	Denzel Washington	Jupiter/Uran (P) Sun/NNode (P)	Sun/NNode Mercury/IC

Sun	RR	Name	Category I Planetary Conjunctions	Category II Special Conjunctions
Sun/Mercury(P) Pisces	AA	Elizabeth Taylor	Venus/Uran (P)	Venus/Uranus/ IC
Sun/Mercury Capricorn	AA	Faye Dunaway	Jupiter/Saturn	Mars/IC
Sun/Mercury Leo	AA	Gene Roddenberry	Moon/Uranus/ Mars/Neptune Jupiter/Saturn	Jupiter/IC
Sun/Mercury Virgo	A	Gretchen Whitmer	Sun/Venus (P) Jupiter/Nept Mars/NNode	Uranus/DSC
Sun/Mercury Gemini	AA	Henry Kissinger		Jupiter/PoF (P) (Neptune/IC)
Sun/Mercury Aries	AA	Helmut Kohl	(Merc/Uranus) Sun/Uranus	Venus/ASC Jupiter/PoF Saturn/MC (P)
Sun/Mercury Virgo	AA	Ingo Swan		Saturn/DSC Uranus/MC Venus/IC
Sun/Mercury(P) Sun/Virgo Mercury/Leo	A	James Van Praagh	Sun/Pluto	NNode/MC (P) PoF/IC Jupiter/MC
Sun/Mercury Scorpio	AA	Jodie Foster	Moon/Uranus Venus/Neptune	
Sun/Mercury Sun/Virgo Mercury/Libra	AA	Julio Iglesias	Sun/Neptune Merc/Nept (P)	Venus/PoF Jupiter/NNode/ MC
Sun/Mercury Sun/Libra Mercury/Scorpio	AA	Kamala Harris	Venus/Pluto Uranus/Pluto	ASC/NNode (Saturn/MC) PoF/DSC
Sun/Mercury Capricorn	A	Lin-Manuel Miranda		Moon/MC (P) Pluto/DSC
Sun/Mercury Leo	AA	Liz Cheney	(Venus/Mars) Uran/Pluto (P)	Jupiter/IC
Sun/Mercury Gemini	AA	Marilyn Monroe		NNode/Pluto
Sun/Mercury (P) Libra	AA	Michelle Mone	Sun/Uranus (P) Merc/Uran (P)	Moon/IC (P)
Sun/Mercury Aquarius	AA	Michio Kaku	Sun/Mars	Uranus/MC (P) Venus/IC (P)

Sun	RR	Name	Category I Planetary Conjunctions	Category II Special Conjunctions
Sun/Mercury Leo	AA	Norman Schwarzkopf	Mars/Pluto (P)	Uranus/MC NNode/DSC
Sun/Mercury (P) Virgo	AA	Oliver Stone		Jupiter/ASC Saturn/MC
Sun/Mercury(P) Pisces	X	Rhonda Byrne	Sun/Jupiter (P) Sun/NNode Mercury/NNode Mercury/Jupiter Jupiter/NNode	
Sun/Mercury Leo	A	Roger Federer	Jupiter/Saturn	
Sun/Mercury(P) Pisces	AA	Ron Howard	Moon/NNode(P)	Sun/Mercury/ PoF Nept/DSC (P) Uranus/IC
Sun/Mercury Aries	AA	Samuel Alito	Sun/NNode Moon/Saturn Venus/Jupiter	Uranus/DSC
Sun/Mercury Pisces	AA	Simone Biles	Sun/Venus Mars/NNode	
Sun/Mercury Leo	A	Sydney Omar	Venus/Pluto (P) Pluto/NNode	NNode/MC
Sun/Mercury Virgo	AA	Tim Burton	Sun/Pluto (P) Venus/Uranus (P) (Jupiter/NNode)	Venus/IC Uranus/IC
Sun/Mercury Taurus	AA	Timothy McVeigh	Venus/Saturn (P) Venus/NNode(P) Saturn/NNode	
Sun/Mercury Aquarius	AA	Tom Brokaw	Mars/Saturn	Jupiter/IC
Sun/Mercury Virgo	AA	Tommy Lee Jones		Pluto/IC (P)
Sun/Venus (P) Cancer	AA	Adam Schiff		NNode/IC Saturn/DSC
Sun/Venus Cancer	A	Alan Turing	Venus/Pluto (P) Sun/Pluto	Jupiter/DSC Uranus/MC

Sun	RR	Name	Category I Planetary Conjunctions	Category II Special Conjunctions
Sun/Venus (P) Aquarius	A	Beatrix of the Netherlands	Sun/Moon Sun/Jupiter Moon/Jupiter (P) Venus/Jupiter (P) Mars/Saturn (P)	
Sun/Venus (P) Virgo	AA	Blake Lively	Sun/Mars (P) Venus/Mars(P)	Pluto/IC (P)
Sun/Venus (P) Aries	AA	Brigette Macron	Sun/Moon Moon/Venus Saturn/Neptune	Jupiter/MC
Sun/Venus Taurus	AA	Carol Burnett		PoF/NNode
Sun/Venus Scorpio	AA	Charles Manson	Mars/Neptune (P) Moon/NNode	Mercury/DSC Jupiter/DSC PoF/IC
Sun/Venus Sagittarius	X	Charles Schulz	Mercury/Venus Moon/Uranus	
Sun/Venus Cancer	X	Dan Aykroyd	Sun/Uranus Moon/Neptune Venus/Uranus	
Sun/Venus Capricorn	AA	David Lynch	Mars/Saturn (P)	Moon/MC
Sun/Venus Scorpio	A	Demi Moore	Mercury/Neptune	PoF/DSC
Sun/Venus Capricorn	AA	Dolly Parton	Mars/Saturn (P)	Uranus/MC (P)
Sun/Venus Aquarius	A	Ellen Degeneris	Mars/Saturn Nept/NNode (P)	
Sun/Venus Aries	AA	George Takei		Mars/MC
Sun/Venus (P) Scorpio	AA	Gordon Ramsay	Moon/Uranus (P)/Pluto	
Sun/Venus (P) Sun/Virgo Venus/Leo	A	Gretchen Whitmer	Sun/Mercury Mars/NNode Jupiter/Neptune	Uranus/DSC
Sun/Venus Sun/Scorpio Venus/Sagittarius	AA	Jamie Lee Curtis	Mercury/Saturn Moon/NNode	Saturn/ASC

Lucky Stars, Lucky Life

Sun	RR	Name	Category I Planetary Conjunctions	Category II Special Conjunctions
Sun/Venus (P) Taurus	AA	Jessica Lange	Sun/NNode Mars/NNode	Mercury/PoF(P) Jupiter/DSC Neptune/IC
Sun/Venus Capricorn	A	Jim Carey	Merc/Jupiter (P)	Uranus/MC Neptune/ASC
Sun/Venus Cancer	AA	Khloe Kardashian	Mars/Saturn Mercury/Venus	Uranus/MC NNode/IC
Sun/Venus (P) Cancer	AA	Leona Helmsley	Sun/Ven/Pluto Mercury/Nept	
Sun/Venus Scorpio	AA	Leonardo DiCaprio	Merc/Uranus (P)	Nept/NNode
Sun/Venus (P) Scorpio	A	Martin Scorsese		NNode/ASC Sun/Venus/IC
Sun/Venus (P) Taurus	AA	Michele Ferrero		NNode/ASC Mercury/MC
Sun/Venus (P) Aquarius	A	Oprah Winfrey		
Sun/Venus Taurus	AA	Pierre Teilhard Chardin	Sun/Neptune Venus/Neptune	
Sun/Venus (P) Aquarius	AA	Rick Warren	Mercury/PoF/ Moon/Mars	Uranus/IC
Sun/Venus Taurus	A	Robert Downey Jr.	Mars/Uranus Uranus/Pluto	Pluto/PoF
Sun/Venus (P) Aquarius	AA	Robert Wagner		Moon/PoF (Neptune/MC)
Sun/Venus (P) Sagittarius	X	Sathya Sai Baba	Sun/Saturn Moon/Pluto Moon/NNode	
Sun/Venus Pisces	AA	Simone Biles	Sun/Mercury Mars/NNode	
Sun/Venus (P) Cancer	B	Wally Amos		
Sun/Venus Taurus	AA	Willie Nelson		Sun/Ven/IC (P) Pluto/DSC (P)
Sun/Mars Pisces	AA	Bernard Anault		Saturn/ASC Moon/MC
Sun/Mars (P) Virgo	AA	Blake Lively	Sun/Venus (P) Venus/Mars (P)	Pluto/IC (P)

Sun	RR	Name	Category I Planetary Conjunctions	Category II Special Conjunctions
Sun/Mars Virgo	AA	Brian De Palma	Merc/Nept (P) Venus/Pluto (P) Jupiter/Saturn	
Sun/Mars (P) Libra	AA	Brie Larson	Saturn/Neptune	Uranus/MC (Saturn/MC) Sun/Mars/DSC
Sun/Mars Virgo	AA	Cameron Diaz		Venus/ASC NNode/DSC
Sun/Mars (P) Scorpio	AA	Danny Divito	Moon/Mercury	
Sun/Mars (P) Capricorn	A	David Bowie	Moon/Saturn	Venus/MC Moon/DSC (P)
Sun/Mars (P) Sagittarius	AA	Dick Clark	Mercury/Mars (P)	Venus/PoF NNode/DSC (P)
Sun/Mars (P) Cancer	AA	Francoise Bettencourt-Meyers	Sun/Mars/Uranus Sun/Uranus (P) Saturn/Nept (P)	Moon/IC
Sun/Mars Taurus	AA	Liberace	Venus/Pluto (P)	Venus/Pluto/DSC Mercury/IC
Sun/Mars (P) Sagittarius	AA	Lucky Luciano	Sun/Moon (P) Sun/Saturn (P) Sun/Uranus Moon/Saturn (P) Mars/Saturn	Sun/Moon/Saturn/MC PoF/ASC
Sun/Mars (P) Aquarius	AA	Michael Bay	Sun/Saturn Mars/Saturn	Mercury/DSC
Sun/Mars Aquarius	AA	Michio Kaku	Sun/Mercury	Uranus/MC (P) Venus/IC (P)
Sun/Mars Taurus	AA	Shirley MacLaine	Moon/Neptune	
Sun/Mars Sun/Sagittarius Mars/Capricorn	AA	Steven Spielberg	Venus/Jupiter	
Sun/Mars (P) Scorpio	AA	Vito Genovese	Sun/Saturn Sun/Uranus (P) Mars/Uranus (P)	

Lucky Stars, Lucky Life

Sun	RR	Name	Category I Planetary Conjunctions	Category II Special Conjunctions
Sun/Jupiter (P) Scorpio	C	Anne Hathaway	Sun/Venus/Jupiter Saturn/Pluto (P) Mercury/Jupiter	
Sun/Jupiter (P) Leo	A	Billy Bob Thorton	Mercury/Jupiter Sun/Mars	
Sun/Jupiter Jupiter/Taurus Sun/Gemini	AA	Bob Dylan	Moon/Saturn Jupiter/Uranus	Mercury/DSC
Sun/Jupiter (P) Capricorn	AA	Donna Summer	Moon/Mars	Saturn/ASC Pluto/PoF
Sun/Jupiter (P) Aquarius	A	Garth Brooks	Sun/Venus Venus/Jupiter Mars/Saturn (P)	Uranus/IC
Sun/Jupiter (P) Aries	AA	James D. Watson	Merc/Venus (P)	Pluto/DSC (P)
Sun/Jupiter Scorpio	AA	Jenifer (Bartoli)	Sun/Venus Sun/Moon/Merc/ Jupiter Saturn/Pluto (P)	
Sun/Jupiter (P) Leo	AA	Joe Rogan	(Uranus/Pluto)	Mercury/IC (P)
Sun/Jupiter Libra	AA	Liliane Bettencourt	Mercury/Saturn	Venus/PoF (P)
Sun/Jupiter Capricorn	AA	Mary Tyler Moore	Moon/Pluto (P)	NNode/MC
Sun/Jupiter Leo	A	Mick Jagger	Sun/Pluto Jupiter/Pluto	Mercury/IC Pluto/IC
Sun/Jupiter (P) Leo	AA	Ray Bradbury	Merc/Neptune Venus/Saturn (P)	(Mars/MC)
Sun/Jupiter (P) Pisces	X	Rhonda Byrne	Sun/Mercury (P) Sun/NNode Mercury/Jupiter Mercury/NNode Jupiter/NNode	
Sun/Jupiter Capricorn	AA	Rod Sterling	Sun/Mercury	NNode/MC
Sun/Saturn (P) Taurus	AA	Al Pacino		NNode/IC

Sun	RR	Name	Category I Planetary Conjunctions	Category II Special Conjunctions
Sun/Saturn Sagittarius	X	Chelsea Manning	Sun/Mercury Sun/Uranus Mercury/Saturn Moon/Mars (P) Moon/Pluto	
Sun/Saturn Pisces	A	Dakota Fanning	Uranus/Neptune Pluto/NNode(P)	Neptune/MC
Sun/Saturn (P) Cancer	AA	Danny Glover	Uran/NNode (P)	
Sun/Saturn Aries	AA	Francis Ford Coppola		Mars/ASC
Sun/Saturn (P) Sagittarius	AA	Lucky Luciano	Sun/Moon (P) Sun/Mars (P) Sun/Uranus Moon/Saturn (P) Mars/Saturn Mars/Uranus	Sun/Moon/ Saturn/MC PoF/ASC
Sun/Saturn Sagittarius	AA	Robert Duvall	Sun/Mercury Mercury/Saturn	
Sun/Saturn Scorpio	AA	Vito Genovese	Sun/Mars (P) Sun/Uranus (P) Mars/Uranus (P)	
Sun/Uranus Leo	AA	Antonio Banderas		Pluto/DSC (P)
Sun/Uranus Sagittarius	X	Chelsea Manning	Sun/Mercury Sun/Saturn Mercury/Saturn Moon/Mars (P) Moon/Pluto	
Sun/Uranus Gemini	AA	Donald Trump	Sun/NNode Venus/Saturn Uran/NNode (P)	Mars/ASC PoF/DSC
Sun/Uranus (P) Cancer	AA	Francoise Bettencourt Meyers	Sun/Mars (P) Sun/Mars/Uranus Saturn/Nept (P)	Moon/IC
Sun/Uranus Aries	AA	Helmut Kohl	Sun/Mercury (Merc/Uranus)	Venus/ASC Jupiter/PoF Saturn/MC (P)
Sun/Uranus (P) Pisces	AA	Jerry Lewis	Venus/Jupiter (P)	Neptune/PoF Sun/Uran/MC

Lucky Stars, Lucky Life

Sun	RR	Name	Category I Planetary Conjunctions	Category II Special Conjunctions
Sun/Uranus (P) Cancer	AA	Meryl Streep	Mercury/Mars	Jupiter/DSC
Sun/Uranus (P) Libra	AA	Michelle Mone	Sun/Mercury (P) Merc/Uranus (P)	Moon/IC (P)
Sun/Uranus Taurus	AA	Rick Nelson	Mercury/Saturn	
Sun/Uranus Gemini	AA	Salman Rushdie	Sun/Moon (P) Moon/Uranus	Mercury/IC PoF/ASC
Sun/Uranus Pisces	C	Sun Myung Moon	Jupiter/Nept (P)	
Sun/Uranus (P) Gemini	AA	Ted Kaczinski	(Mercury/Jupiter) Sun/Saturn (P) Saturn/Uranus	Merc/ASC (P) NNode/PoF
Sun/Neptune (P) Sagittarius	AA	Christina Applegate	Moon/Mars Mercury/Venus	
Sun/Neptune Libra	AA	Claude Vorhilon (Rael)	Mars/Jupiter	NNode/MC (P)
Sun/Neptune Taurus	AA	Pierre Teilhard de Chardin	Sun/Venus Venus/Neptune	
Sun/Neptune Virgo	AA	Sean Connery		Saturn/ASC
Sun/Neptune Virgo	A	Warren Buffet		(Venus/MC)
Sun/Pluto Cancer	A	Alan Turing	Sun/Venus Venus/Pluto (P)	Jupiter/DSC Uranus/MC
Sun/Pluto Cancer	AA	Gina Lollobrigida	Venus/Neptune Jupiter/Uran (P)	Neptune/IC
Sun/Pluto Cancer	AA	Janet Leigh	Jupiter/Uran (P)	Mars/MC
Sun/Pluto (P) Scorpio	AA	Katy Perry	Moon/Saturn (P)	Mercury/ASC
Sun/Pluto (P) Cancer	AA	Merv Griffin	Moon/Jupiter (P) Mercury/Venus Venus/Mars/ NNode	Uranus/MC Pluto/ASC
Sun/Pluto (P) Gemini	AA	Padre Pio	Mars/Nept (P)	

Sun	RR	Name	Category I Planetary Conjunctions	Category II Special Conjunctions
Sun/Pluto (P) Virgo	AA	Tim Burton	Sun/Mercury (P) Venus/Uran (P) (Jupiter/NNode.)	Venus/IC Uranus/IC
Sun/ASC (P) Sagittarius	AA	Bruce Lee	Venus/Mars Jupiter/Saturn	Moon/PoF (P)
Sun/ASC Virgo	AA	David Copperfield	Venus/Uranus	Moon/PoF
Sun/ASC (P) Cancer	AA	Imelda Marcos	Mars/Nept (P) Venus/NNode	
Sun/ASC Gemini	AA	Steffi Graf	Venus/Saturn (Jupiter/Uranus)	Moon/PoF
Sun/ASC (P) Aquarius	AA	Wayne Gretsky	Jupiter/Saturn Pluto/NNode (P)	
Sun/MC Libra	AA	Johnny Mathis		NNode/PoF
Sun/MC (P) Gemini	AA	Kirk Kerkorian	Mercury/Mars/Jupiter Mars/Jupiter (P)	

Moon	RR	Name	Category I Planetary Conjunctions	Category II Planetary Conjunctions
Moon/Mercury Aquarius	A	Andrew Yang	Moon/Mercury Mercury/Venus Neptune/NNode	Mars/PoF Uranus/MC
Moon/Merc (P) Aquarius	AA	Clint Black	Sun/Moon (P) Sun/Mercury Mercury/Venus Venus/Jupiter (P) Mars/Saturn	Pluto/PoF PoF/ASC
Moon/Mercury Aquarius	AA	Eddie Van Halen		Sun/IC Nept/ASC (P)
Moon/Merc (P) Leo	A	Halle Berry	Mars/Jupiter Uranus/Pluto (P)	NNode/ASC Venus/IC
Moon/Mercury Aquarius	AA	Michael Bloomberg	Mars/Saturn Saturn/Uranus	

Moon	RR	Name	Category I Planetary Conjunctions	Category II Special Conjunctions
Moon/Merc(P) Scorpio	AA	Miley Cyrus	Moon/Mercury/ Pluto Venus/Uranus Uranus/Neptune	Sun/Moon/ Mercury/DSC Merc/DSC (P)
Moon/Mercury Aquarius	AA	Muhammad Ali		Venus/DSC (P) Pluto/PoF (P)
Moon/Mercury Libra	DD	Niels Bohr	Moon/Uranus (P) Jupiter/NNode	
Moon/Mercury Leo	A	Ringo Starr	Jupiter/Saturn Moon/Mercury/ Mars/Pluto (P)	Neptune/DSC Venus/IC
Moon/Mercury Scorpio	AA	Whoopi Goldberg	Sun/Saturn Jupiter/Pluto	Venus/MC
Moon/Venus Taurus	AA	Billy Crystal	Mars/Saturn Saturn/Pluto	Moon/ASC
Moon/Venus (P) Taurus	AA	Mackenzie Scott	Moon/Mercury Moon/Saturn	Mercury/ASC
Moon/Venus (P) Virgo	A	Rachael Ray	Mercury/Venus Moon/Pluto	Uranus/PoF Jupiter/ASC
Moon/Venus Cancer	A	Sydney Omar	Sun/Mercury	NNode/MC
Moon/Mars Aries	AA	Angelina Jolie	Moon/Jupiter	Venus/ASC (P) Jupiter/MC (P)
Moon/Mars Moon/Aries Mars/Taurus	A	Celine Dion	Merc/Venus(P) Sun/Saturn Saturn/NNode	Sun/MC Saturn/MC NNode/MC
Moon/Mars Pisces	AA	Christina Applegate	Sun/Neptune (P) Mercury/Venus	
Moon/Mars Cancer	AA	Liza Minnelli	Moon/Mars/ Saturn	Moon/Mars/ Saturn/IC
Moon/Mars Cancer	AA	Nancy Sinatra	Venus/Mars (P)	Pluto/IC NNode/IC
Moon/Mars (P) Sagittarius	DD	Recep Erdogan	Merc/Venus (P)	
Moon/Mars Pisces	AA	Ricky Martin	Venus/NNode	Jupiter/DSC (P)
Moon/Jupiter Taurus	A	Ann Margret	Sun/Venus Moon/Uranus (P)	

Moon	RR	Name	Category I Special Conjunctions	Category II Special Conjunctions
Moon/Jupiter Moon/Cap Jupiter/Sag	AA	Al Gore	Mars/Saturn	
Moon/Jupiter	A	Ariana Grande	Uranus/Nept (P)	
Moon/Jupiter Libra	AA	George W Bush	Mercury/Pluto NNode/Uranus	Mercury/ASC
Moon/Jupiter Cancer	AA	Jimi Hendrix	Sun/Venus Sun/Mercury	
Moon/Jup (P) Capricorn	AA	Merv Grifffen	Sun/Pluto (P) Mercury/Venus Venus/Mars/ NNode	Sun/Pluto/AC
Moon/Jup (P) Scorpio	A	Mitt Romney		Moon/Jup/DSC Venus/PoF(P)/ MC
Moon/Jup (P) Libra	AA	Tyler Perry	Sun/Pluto Moon/Mercury	
Moon/Jupiter Aries	AA	Whitney Houston	Merc/Pluto (P)	Merc/Pluto/DSC
Moon/Saturn Cancer	AA	Augusto Pinochet	Uranus/NNode	
Moon/Saturn Taurus	AA	Bob Dylan	Sun/Jupiter Jupiter/Uranus	Mercury/DSC
Moon/Saturn Scorpio	AA	Chris Evert	Sun/Mercury Moon/Venus Venus/Saturn Jupiter/Uranus	Pluto/MC NNode/PoF
Moon/Saturn Aquarius	AA	Conan O'Brien		Uranus/ASC
Moon/Saturn Leo	A	David Bowie	Sun/Mars (P)	Venus/MC Moon/DSC
Moon/Saturn Capricorn	AA	George Clooney	Pluto/NNode	
Moon/Sat (P) Pisces	AA	Herb Alpert		Pluto/PoF Jupiter/IC
Moon/Sat (P) Scorpio	AA	Katy Perry	Sun/Pluto (P)	Mercury/ASC NNode/PoF

Lucky Stars, Lucky Life

Moon	RR	Name	Category I Planetary Conjunctions	Category II Planetary Conjunctions
Moon/Sat (P) Sagittarius	AA	Lucky Luciano	Sun/Moon (P) Sun/Mars (P) Sun/Saturn (P) Sun/Uranus Mars/Saturn Mars/Uranus	Sun/Moon/ Saturn/MC PoF/ASC
Moon/Saturn Capricorn	AA	Willie Mays	Venus/NNode (P)	Mercury/PoF
Moon/Uran (P) Taurus	A	Ann-Margret	Sun/Venus Moon/Jup/Uran	
Moon/Uranus Pisces	X	Charles Schultz	Sun/Venus Mercury/Venus	
Moon/Uran (P) Virgo	AA	Gordon Ramsay	Sun/Venus (P) Moon/Pluto Mars/Pluto	
Moon/Uranus Aries	AA	Jim Jones	Moon/NNode	
Moon/Uranus Virgo	AA	Jodie Foster	Sun/Mercury Venus/Neptune	
Moon/Uranus	A	Joe Montana	Jupiter/Pluto (P)	Saturn/PoF (P)
Moon/Uran (P) Libra	DD	Niels Bohr	Moon/Mercury Jupiter/NNode	
Moon/Uranus Cancer	A	Oliva Newton-John	Venus/Pluto	Jupiter/PoF (P) Jupiter/PoF/IC
Moon/Uranus Aquarius	AA	Orson Wells	Moon/NNode Saturn/Pluto	
Moon/Uranus Gemini	A	Salman Rushdie	Sun/Moon (P) Sun/Uranus	Mercury/IC PoF/ASC Jupiter/ASC (P)
Moon/Nept (P) Virgo	AA	Dustin Hoffman		Jupiter/ASC (P)
Moon/Nept (P) Capricorn	AA	Justin Timberlake	Jupiter/Sat (P)	Mars/DSC (P) Jupiter/PoF
Moon/Neptune Virgo	AA	Shirley MacLaine	Sun/Mars	
Moon/Pluto (P) Cancer	AA	Mary Tyler Moore	Sun/Jupiter	NNode/MC

Moon	RR	Name	Category I Planetary Conjunctions	Category II Planetary Conjunctions
Moon/Pluto Cancer	X	Sathya Sai Baba	Sun/Venus (P) Sun/Saturn Moon/Pluto Moon/NNode	
Moon/Pluto Capricorn	AA	Ted Danson	Sun/Mercury	Uranus/MC
Moon/ASC Taurus	AA	Dione Warrick	Jupiter/Saturn	Pluto/IC
Moon/ASC Scorpio	AA	James Caan	Venus/Uranus	Mars/DSC
Moon/ASC (P) Taurus	AA	Sigourney Weaver	Sun/Neptune (P) Mars/Pluto	Sun/PoF (P) Neptune/PoF Jupiter/MC
Moon/MC Taurus	AA	Berhnard Arnault	Sun/Mars	Saturn/ASC
Moon/MC (P) Virgo	AA	David Lynch	Sun/Venus Mars/Saturn (P)	
Moon/MC Gemini	AA	Doris Day		Mercury/DSC
Moon/MC Virgo	A	Keith Richards	Mars/Uranus Pluto/NNode	PoF/IC
Moon/MC (P) Capricorn	AA	Lin-Manuel Miranda	Sun/Mercury	Pluto/DSC
Moon/MC (P)	AA	Lucky Luciano	Sun/Moon(P) Sun/Mars (P) Sun/Saturn (P) Sun/Uranus Moon/Saturn (P) Mars/Saturn Mars/Uranus	PoF/ASC Sun/MC Saturn/MC
Moon/MC Sagittarius	AA	Patti Davis	Moon/Venus Saturn/Neptune	Moon/MC NNode/ASC
Moon/MC (P) Libra	AA	Sylvester Stallone	Moon/Jupiter Merc/Pluto (P) Uran/NNode (P)	Jupiter/MC

Lucky Stars, Lucky Life

Mercury	RR	Name	Category I Planetary Conjunctions	Category II Planetary Conjunctions
Mercury/Venus	A	Andrew Yang	Moon/Mercury Neptune/NNode	Mars/PoF Uranus/MC
Merc/Venus (P)	AA	Clint Black	Sun/Moon Moon/Merc (P) Venus/Jupiter (P) Mars/Saturn	Pluto/PoF PoF/ASC
Mercury/Venus	AA	Gene Wilder	Mars/Jupiter	Saturn/MC (P)
Merc/Venus (P)	AA	J. B. Pritzker	Uranus/Pluto	
Mercury/Venus	AA	James D. Watson	Sun/Jupiter (P)	Pluto/DSC
Merc/Venus (P)	A	Joan Rivers	Mars/Jupiter	
Mercury/Venus	AA	Johnny Depp	Mars/Uranus	
Merc/Venus (P)		Kathy Bates	(Mercury/Uranus)	Moon/DSC Jupiter/IC Uranus/MC
Mercury/Venus	AA	Paul Newman		Merc/ASC (P) Venus/ASC (Pluto/DSC)
Mercury/Venus	AA	Princess Stephanie of Monaco	Sun/Moon Uranus/Pluto	Jupiter/MC PoF/ASC
Merc/Venus (P)	DD	Recep Erdogan	Moon/Mars (P)	
Mercury/Mars	AA	Cindy Crawford	Sun/Moon Mars/Saturn (P) Uranus/Pluto (P) Mercury/Mars	
Mercury/Mars	AA	Dean Martin	Mercury/Jupiter Mars/Jupiter (P)	
Mercury/Mars (P)	AA	Dick Clark	Sun/Mars (P) Sun/Merc/Mars	Venus/PoF NNode/DSC
Mercury/Mars	AA	Heather Locklear	Venus/Uranus Jupiter/Saturn Uranus/NNode	Sun/DSC Mars/PoF
Mercury/Mars	AA	Lamar Kendrick		Jupiter/DSC Merc/PoF (P) Mars/PoF (P)

Mercury	RR	Name	Category I Planetary Conjunctions	Category II Planetary Conjunctions
Merc/Mars (P)	A	Orlando Bloom	Moon/NNode (P)	Neptune/MC
Mercury/Mars	AA	Raquel Welch	Sun/Merc/Mars Jupiter/Saturn (P)	
Mercury/Jupiter	A	Billy Bob Thorton	Sun/Jupiter (P) Venus/Uranus	
Mercury/Jup (P)	AA	Brigette Bardot		Mars/PoF Moon/DSC
Mercury/Jupiter	AA	Dean Martin	Mercury/Mars Mars/Jupiter (P)	
Mercury/Jup (P)	A	Jim Carey	Sun/Venus Sun/Saturn	Neptune/ASC Uranus/MC
Mercury/Jup (P)	AA	Karen Carpenter	Moon/Pluto	Uranus/ASC
Mercury/Jup	AA	Kevin Hart	Saturn/NNode/ ASC	Mars/MC Moon/IC
Mercury/Jup (P)	AA	Woody Allen	Sun/Merc/Jupiter	Saturn/DSC
Mercury/Saturn	AA	Albert Einstein		Mercury/PoF (P)
Mercury/Saturn	AA	Bo Derek	Sun/NNode (P)	Moon/IC
Mercury/Saturn	AA	Peter Hurkos	Mercury/NNode.	Pluto/ASC
Mercury/Saturn	AA	Rick Nelson	Sun/Uranus	
Mercury/Saturn	AA	Robert Duvall	Sun/Saturn (P)	
Mercury/Saturn	AA	Sonny Bono	Sun/Mercury (P)	
Mercury/Sat (P)	A	Wayne Dyer	Sun/Uranus Moon/Mars	Mars/IC Venus/IC
Merc/Uran (P)	AA	Adam Driver		Merc/Uran/MC NNode/IC
Mercury/Uranus	AA	Gwen Stefani		Moon/DSC Saturn/IC
Mercury/Uranus	AA	Kathy Bates	Merc/Venus (P)	Uranus/MC Moon/DSC Jupiter/IC
Mercury/Uranus	AA	Lebron James		Mars/MC Neptune/DSC

Mercury	RR	Name	Category I Planetary Conjunctions	Category II Planetary Conjunctions
Merc/Uran (P)	AA	Leonardo DiCaprio	Sun/Venus (P) Neptune/NNode	Mars/PoF
Merc/Uran (P)	AA	Michelle Mone	Sun/Mercury (P) Sun/Uranus (P)	Moon/IC (P)
Merc/Nept (P)	AA	Brian de Palma	Sun/Mars Venus/Pluto (P) Jupiter/Saturn	
Mercury/Neptune	A	Christina Aguillera	Sun/Neptune Venus/Uranus Jupiter/Saturn (P)	
Merc/Nept (P)	AA	Jake Gyllenhaal	Jupiter/Saturn (P)	NNode/ASC
Merc/Nept (P)	AA	Julio Iglesias	Sun/Merc/Nept	Venus/PoF Jupiter/MC (P) NNode/MC
Mercury/Neptune	AA	Kris Jenner	Jupiter/Pluto (P)	
Merc/Nept (P)	AA	Maria Shriver	Jupiter/Pluto (P)	Jup/Pluto/PoF Uranus/IC
Merc/Nept (P)	A	Meg Ryan	Mercury/Venus/ Neptune	Venus/Nept/ MC
Mercury/Neptune	AA	Robert Redford	Moon/Merc (P) Moon/Merc/Nept	NNode/MC
Mercury/Neptune	AA	Ru Paul	Moon/Merc/Nept	Venus/Jup/DSC Pluto/NNode/ IC
Mercury/Pluto (P)	AA	George W Bush	Moon/Jupiter Uran/NNode (P)	Mercury/ASC
Mercury/Pluto (P)	AA	James Brolin	Jupiter/Saturn	NNode/ASC
Mercury/Pluto (P)	AA	Sylvester Stallone	Uran/NNode (P)	Moon/MC (P) Jupiter/MC
Mercury/Pluto (P)	AA	Whitney Houston	Moon/Jupiter	Mercury/Pluto/ DSC
Mercury/ASC (P)	AA	Paul Newman	Mercury/Venus	Venus/ASC (Pluto/DSC)

Mercury	RR	Name	Category I Planetary Conjunctions	Category II Planetary Conjunctions
Merc/ASC (P)	AA	Ted Kaczynski	Sun/Uranus (P) Sun/Saturn (P) (Mercury/Jupiter) Saturn/Uranus	NNode/PoF
Mercury/ASC	AA	Katy Perry	Moon/Saturn (P)	
Mercury/MC (P)	AA	Henry Winkler	Venus/Jupiter (P) Mars/Saturn	

Venus	RR	Name	Category I Planetary Conjunctions	Category II Planetary Conjunctions
Venus/Mars	AA	Barry Bonds		PoF/Mars/DSC
Venus/Mars (P)	AA	Blake Livley	Sun/Venus (P) Sun/Mars (P)	Pluto/IC
Venus/Mars (P)	AA	Cristiano Ronaldo		Nept/ASC (P)
Venus/Mars	AA	Dwayne Johnson		Mercury/DSC Saturn/PoF
Venus/Mars	AA	Michael Crichton		PoF/DSC (P)
Venus/Mars (P)	AA	Zendaya		Mercury/PoF
Venus/Jup (P)	A	Beatrix of the Netherlands	Sun/Venus (P) Moon/Jupiter (P) Mars/Saturn (P)	
Venus/Jup (P)	AA	Clint Black	Sun/Moon (P) Moon/Merc (P) Mercury/Jupiter Merc/Venus (P) Mars/Saturn	PoF/ASC (Pluto/PoF)
Venus/Jupiter	A	Garth Brooks	Sun/Jupiter (P) Mars/Saturn (P)	Uranus/IC
Venus/Jup (P)	AA	Henry Winkler	Mars/Saturn	Merc/MC (P)
Venus/Jupiter	AA	Jennifer Lawrence		Mercury/MC
Venus/Jup (P)	AA	Jerry Lewis	Sun/Uranus (P)	Neptune/PoF Sun/Uran/MC

Venus	RR	Name	Category I Planetary Conjunctions	Category II Planetary Conjunctions
Venus/Jup (P)	AA	Roman Polanski		Moon/MC Neptune/PoF
Venus/Saturn	A	Bill Gates	Jupiter/Pluto (P)	Moon/MC
Venus/Saturn	AA	Chris Evert	Sun/Mercury Moon/Saturn Moon/Venus Jupiter/Uranus	Pluto/MC NNode/PoF
Venus/Saturn	AA	Donald Trump	Sun/Uranus Sun/NNode Uranus/NNode	Mars/ASC PoF/DSC
Venus/Saturn	AA	Kurt Cobain		Uran/Plut/ASC Venus/DSC PoF/NNode
Venus/Saturn	AA	Nicholas Cage		Jupiter/IC
Venus/Sat (P)	AA	Ray Bradbury	Sun/Jupiter (P) Mercury/Neptune	(Mars/MC)
Venus/Saturn	AA	Steffi Graff	(Jupiter/Uranus)	Sun/ASC Moon/PoF
Venus/Saturn (P)	AA	Timothy McVeigh	Sun/Mercury Venus/NNode (P)	
Venus/Uranus	AA	Candice Bergen	Mars/Pluto	Jupiter/MC (P)
Venus/Uranus (P)	AA	Elizabeth Taylor	Sun/Mercury (P)	
Venus/Uranus (P)	AA	Pat Boone		Mars/DSC Neptune/MC
Venus/Uranus (P)	AA	Tim Burton	Sun/Mercury Sun/Pluto (P) (Jupiter/NNode)	Venus/IC Uranus/IC
Venus/Uranus	AA	Warren Beatty		Saturn/DSC
Venus/Neptune	AA	Jimmy Carter	Venus/NNode Nept/NNode (P)	
Venus/Neptune	AA	Jodie Foster	Sun/Mercury Moon/Uranus	
Venus/Neptune	AA	Leonard Cohen		Sun/ASC/ Moon/PoF

Venus	RR	Name	Category I Planetary Conjunctions	Category II Planetary Conjunctions
Venus/Neptune	A	Meg Ryan		Merc/Venus/Neptune/MC
Venus/Neptune	AA	Pierre Teilhard de Chardin	Sun/Venus Sun/Neptune	
Venus/Neptune	AA	Teri Hatcher	Mars/Uranus (P) Mars/Pluto (P) Uranus/Pluto	
Venus/Pluto (P)	AA	Brian de Palma	Sun/Mars Mercury/Nept (P) Jupiter/Saturn	
Venus/Pluto (P)	AA	Guglielmo Marconi	Sun/NNode (P)	Jupiter/IC
Venus/Pluto	AA	Jeffree Star	Mercury/Uranus	Mars/MC Jupiter/PoF
Venus/Pluto (P)	AA	Joseph Di Mambro	Sun/NNode Neptune/NNode	Mercury/PoF
Venus/Pluto	AA	Kamala Harris	Sun/Mercury Uranus/Pluto	NNode/ASC PoF/DSC Saturn/MC
Venus/Pluto (P)	AA	Kendall Jenner	Uran/Neptune Mercury/NNode	
Venus/Pluto (P)	AA	Liberace	Sun/Mars	Venus/Pluto/DSC
Venus/Pluto	A	Olivia Newton John	Moon/Uranus Mercury/Venus	Jupiter/IC/PoF
Venus/Pluto	A	Rachel Ray	Moon/Venus/Pluto Mercury/Venus	Jupiter/ASC
Venus/Pluto (P)	A	Sydney Omar	Sun/Mercury Moon/Venus Pluto/NNode	NNode/MC
Venus/ASC (P)	AA	Angelina Jolie	Moon/Mars	Jupiter/MC (P)
Venus/ASC	AA	Ben Affleck		
Venus/ASC	AA	Cameron Diaz	Sun/Mars	NNode/DSC
Venus/ASC	AA	Helmut Kohl	Sun/Mercury Sun/Uranus Mercury/Uranus	Jupiter/PoF

Venus	RR	Name	Category I Planetary Conjunctions	Category II Planetary Conjunctions
Venus/ASC	AA	Kiefer Sutherland	Uranus/Pluto	NNode/IC
Venus/ASC	AA	Pierre Omidyar	Uranus/Pluto	

Mars	RR	Name	Category I Planetary Conjunctions	Category II Planetary Conjunctions
Mars/Jup (P)	AA	Amelia Earhart	Moon/Pluto Venus/Jupiter (P) Saturn/Uranus (P)	Neptune/PoF
Mars/Jupiter	AA	Bon Jovi		Moon/IC
Mars/Jupiter	AA	Claude Vorilhon (Rael)	Sun/Neptune	NNode/MC (P)
Mars/Jup (P)	AA	Dean Martin	Mercury/Mars Mercury/Jupiter	
Mars/Jupiter	AA	Eldridge Cleaver		Pluto/ASC NNode/DSC
Mars/Jupiter	AA	Gene Wilder	Mercury/Venus	Saturn/MC (P)
Mars/Jup (P)	AA	Kirk Kerkorian	Merc/Mars/Jup	Sun/MC (P)
Mars/Jupiter	AA	Queen Elizabeth II		Saturn/MC
Mars/Jupiter (P)	AA	Willem Dafoe	Sun/Uranus	Sun/DSC
Mars/Saturn	AA	Al Gore	Moon/Jupiter	
Mars/Saturn (P)	AA	Cindy Crawford	Sun/Moon Mercury/Mars Uranus/Pluto (P)	
Mars/Saturn (P)	AA	David Lynch	Sun/Venus	Moon/MC (P)
Mars/Saturn (P)	AA	Dolly Parton	Sun/Venus	Uran/MC (P)
Mars/Saturn	AA	Ellen DeGeneres	Sun/Venus Nept/NNode (P)	
Mars/Saturn (P)	A	Garth Brooks	Sun/Mercury Sun/Jupiter (P) Venus/Jupiter	Uranus/IC
Mars/Saturn	AA	Khloe Kardashian	Sun/Venus Mercury/Venus	Uranus/MC NNode/IC

Mars	RR	Name	Category I Planetary Conjunctions	Category II Planetary Conjunctions
Mars/Saturn	AA	Michael Bay	Sun/Mars (P)	Mercury/DSC
Mars/Saturn (P)	AA	Paris Jackson	Sun/Jupiter (P)	
Mars/Saturn	AA	Penelope Cruz		Mercury/ASC Uranus/DSC
Mars/Saturn	AA	Tom Brokaw	Sun/Mercury Sun/Saturn	Jupiter/IC
Mars/Uranus	A	Arnold Schwarzenegger	Sun/Saturn Saturn/Pluto	
Mars/Uranus (P)	AA	Gloria Gaynor	Sun/Venus	
Mars/Uranus	AA	H. G. Wells	Sun/NNode	Mars/PoF (P)
Mars/Uranus (P)	DD	Joe Frazier	Pluto/NNode	Mars/Uran/PoF
Mars/Uranus (P)	AA	John Denver	NNode/Pluto	
Mars/Uranus	AA	Robin Williams	Moon/NNode (P)	Merc/MC (P)
Mars/Uranus	C	Ryan Reynolds	Sun/NNode Moon/NNode (P) Moon/Uranus	
Mars/Uran (P)	AA	Teri Hatcher	Venus/Neptune Mars/Pluto (P) Uranus/Pluto	
Mars/Uran (P)	AA	Vito Genovese	Sun/Mars (P) Sun/Uranus (P)	
Mars/Neptune	A	Billy Idol	Sun/Mercury Jupiter/Pluto	Saturn/PoF Uranus/IC
Mars/Neptune	AA	Carl Sagan	Sun/Venus Mercury/Jupiter	NNode/MC (P)
Mars/Nept (P)	AA	Charles Manson	Sun/Venus Moon/NNode (P)	Mercury/DSC Jupiter/DSC PoF/IC
Mars/Neptune	AA	Dane Rudhyar	Mars/Pluto	Neptune/DSC
Mars/Nept (P)	AA	Imelda Marcos	Venus/NNode	Sun/ASC (P)
Mars/Pluto	AA	Brian Wilson	Sun/Jupiter Saturn/Uranus	

Mars	RR	Name	Category I Planetary Conjunctions	Category II Planetary Conjunctions
Mars/Pluto	AA	Gordon Ramsay	Sun/Venus Moon/Uranus Moon/Pluto	
Mars/Pluto (P)	AA	Norman Schwarzkopf	Sun/Mercury	Uranus/MC NNode/DSC
Mars/Pluto (P)	A	Ringo Starr	Moon/Mars/Pluto Jupiter/Saturn	
Mars/Pluto (P)	AA	Teri Hatcher	Venus/Neptune Mars/Uranus (P) Uranus/Pluto	
Mars/ASC (P)	AA	Bob Barker		Neptune/MC Moon/IC NNode/PoF
Mars/ASC	AA	Donald Trump	Sun/Uranus Sun/NNode Uranus/NNode Venus/Saturn	
Mars/ASC	AA	Francis Ford Coppola	Sun/Saturn	
Mars/ASC	AA	Tony Blair	Saturn/Nept (P)	Moon/NNode
Mars/MC	AA	George Takei	Sun/Venus	
Mars/MC	AA	Janet Leigh	Sun/Pluto Jupiter/Uran (P)	
Mars/MC	AA	Jeffree Starr	Venus/Pluto Mercury/Uranus	Jupiter/PoF
Mars/MC	AA	Kevin Hart	Mercury/Jupiter	Moon/IC Saturn/ASC
Mars/MC	AA	Kylie Jenner	Venus/NNode	
Mars/MC	AA	Lebron James	Mercury/Uranus	Neptune/DSC
Jupiter	**RR**	**Name**	**Category I Planetary Conjunctions**	**Category II Planetary Conjunctions**
Jupiter/Saturn	AA	Adriana Lima		Sun/DSC
Jupiter/Saturn (P)	A	Alex Trebek	Sun/Mercury (P) Sun/Pluto	

Jupiter	RR	Name	Category I Planetary Conjunctions	Category II Planetary Conjunctions
Jupiter/Saturn (P)	C	Alicia Keys	Mercury/Mars Moon/Jup/Saturn	
Jupiter/Saturn	AA	Bernardo Bertolucci		Nept/ASC (P) Sun/DSC (P)
Jupiter/Saturn	AA	Brian de Palma	Sun/Mars Mercury/Nept (P) Venus/Pluto (P)	Mars/DSC (P)
Jupiter/Saturn	AA	Bruce Lee	Venus/Mars	Moon/PoF Uranus/ASC
Jupiter/Saturn (P)	A	Christina Aguilera	Sun/Neptune Mercury/Neptune Venus/Uranus	
Jupiter/Saturn (P)	AA	Clara Morgane	Mercury/Mars (P)	NNode/MC (P)
Jupiter/Saturn	AA	Dione Warwick		Moon/ASC Pluto/IC
Jupiter/Saturn	AA	Faye Dunaway	Sun/Mercury	Mars/IC
Jupiter/Saturn	AA	Gene Roddenberry	Sun/Mercury Moon/Uranus Mars/Neptune	
Jupiter/Saturn (P)	AA	George Stephanopolous	Pluto/NNode (P)	Mercury/PoF Saturn/MC (P)
Jupiter/Saturn (P)	AA	Jake Gyllenhaal	Mercury/Nept (P)	NNode/ASC (P)
Jupiter/Saturn	AA	James Brolin	Merc/Pluto(P)	NNode/ASC Moon/DSC Uranus/IC
Jupiter/Saturn	AA	Joan Baez	Sun/Mercury	
Jupiter/Saturn (P)	A	John Lennon	Sun/DSC	
Jupiter/Saturn (P)	AA	Joseph Gordon-Levitt	Sun/Mercury (P) Moon/NNode	
Jupiter/Saturn (P)	AA	Justin Timberlake	Moon/Nept (P)	Jupiter/PoF Mars/DSC
Jupiter/Saturn (P)	AA	Martin Sheen	Sun/Moon	Mars/DSC PoF/ASC

Jupiter	RR	Name	Category I Planetary Conjunctions	Category II Planetary Conjunctions
Jupiter/Saturn (P)	AA	Meghan, Duchess of Sussex	Moon/Jupiter Moon/Saturn (P)	
Jupiter/Saturn (P)	A	Nayib Bukele	Sun/NNode (P)	
Jupiter/Saturn (P)	AA	Nick Nolte		Jupiter/ASC (P) Saturn/ASC Neptune/PoF
Jupiter/Saturn (P)	C	Paris Hilton	Sun/Mercury (P) Moon/NNode	
Jupiter/Saturn (P)	AA	Pele	Mars/NNode (P)	
Jupiter/Saturn	AA	Placido Domingo		Mars/IC
Jupiter/Saturn	AA	Rami Malek		Moon/IC Pluto/PoF
Jupiter/Saturn (P)	AA	Raquel Welch	Sun/Mercury Sun/Mars	
Jupiter/Saturn	AA	Richard Pryor	Venus/Mars (P)	
Jupiter/Saturn	AA	Ringo Starr	Mars/Pluto (P) Moon/Mercury/ Mars/Pluto	
Jupiter/Saturn	AA	Wayne Gretzky	Pluto/NNode (P)	Sun/ASC
Jupiter/Uranus	AA	Bob Dylan	Sun/Jupiter Moon/Saturn	Mercury/DSC
Jupiter/Uranus	AA	Chris Evert	Sun/Mercury Moon/Saturn Moon/Venus Venus/Saturn	Pluto/MC NNode/PoF
Jupiter/Uran (P)	AA	Denzel Washington	Sun/Mercury	Sun/NNode/ Mercury/IC (P)
Jupiter/Uran (P)	AA	Donald Glover	Venus/Mars	NNode/Mars
Jupiter/Uranus	AA	Eddie Van Halen	Moon/Mercury	Sun/IC Nept/ASC (P)
Jupiter/Uran (P)	AA	Gina Llobrigida	Venus/Neptune	Neptune/IC
Jupiter/Uran (P)	AA	Janet Leigh	Sun/Pluto	Mars/MC

Jupiter	RR	Name	Category I Planetary Conjunctions	Category II Planetary Conjunctions
Jupiter/Uranus	AA	Jennifer Aniston		Mercury/IC Saturn/DSC Moon/PoF Saturn/PoF
Jupiter/Uranus	AA	Kevin Costner		Saturn/PoF.
Jupiter/Neptune	AA	Audrey Hepburn	(Mars/Uranus)	Mercury/DSC
Jupiter/Neptune	A	Gretchen Whitmer	Sun/Mercury Sun/Venus/(P) Jupiter/Neptune Mars/NNode	Uranus/DSC
Jupiter/Neptune	AA	Mark Wahlberg	Mercury/Saturn NNode/Mars	Nept/PoF (P) Jupiter/Nept
Jupiter/Nept (P)	C	Sun Myung Moon	Sun/Uranus	
Jupiter/Pluto	A	Anthony Bourdain		Neptune/IC
Jupiter/Pluto	AA	Arsenio Hall	Sun/Moon	Venus/IC
Jupiter/Pluto (P)	A	Bill Gates	Venus/Saturn	Moon/MC
Jupiter/Pluto	AA	Bill Maher	Mars/Saturn	PoF/MC
Jupiter/Pluto	A	Billy Idol	Sun/Mercury Mars/Neptune	Saturn/PoF Uranus/IC
Jupiter/Pluto	AA	Jim Jones	Moon/NNode Moon/Uranus	
Jupiter/Pluto (P)	A	Joe Montana	Moon/Uranus	Saturn/PoF (P)
Jupiter/Pluto (P)	X	Ken Griffen	Sun/Mercury (P)	
Jupiter/Pluto (P)	AA	Kris Jenner	Mercury/Neptune	
Jupiter/Pluto (P)	AA	Maria Shriver	Mercury/Neptune	Jup/Pluto/PoF Uranus/IC
Jupiter/Pluto	AA	Marshall Applewhite	Sun/Moon (NNode/Uranus)	PoF/ASC
Jupiter/Pluto	AA	Tom Hanks		Venus/MC Mars/DSC
Jupiter/ASC	AA	Dustin Hoffman	Moon/Nept (P)	

Jupiter	RR	Name	Category I Planetary Conjunctions	Category II Planetary Conjunctions
Jupiter/ASC	AA	Jane Fonda		Neptune/PoF Pluto/DSC
Jupiter/ASC	AA	Trisha Yearwood	Sun/Mercury (P) Sun/Uranus (P) Merc/Uranus (P)	Moon/IC (P)
Jupiter/MC (P)	AA	Angelina Jolie	Moon/Mars Moon/Jupiter	Venus/ASC
Jupiter/MC	AA	Brigette Macron	Sun/Moon Sun/Venus (P) Moon/Venus Saturn/Neptune	
Jupiter/MC (P)	AA	Candice Bergen	Venus/Uranus Mars/Pluto	
Jupiter/MC	AA	Goldie Hawn	Moon/NNode	Saturn/PoF (P) Moon/DSC
Jupiter/MC (P)	AA	Julio Iglesias	Sun/Merc/Nept Mercury/Nept (P)	Venus/PoF NNode/MC
Jupiter/MC (P)	AA	Kim Kardashian		Moon/IC (P)
Jupiter/MC	AA	Michael Jordan		Venus/DSC (P)
Jupiter/MC	AA	Michel Gauquelin		Mercury/IC
Jupiter/MC	AA	Princess Stephanie of Monaco	Mercury/Venus Uranus/Pluto	PoF/ASC
Jupiter/MC	AA	Sigourney Weaver	Sun/Neptune (P) Mars/Pluto	Moon/ASC Sun/Nept/PoF
Jupiter/MC	AA	Slyvester Stallone	Moon/Jupiter Mercury/Pluto (P)	Moon/MC (P)
Jupiter/MC	AA	William, Prince of Wales	Sun/Moon	Sun/DSC Neptune/ASC
Jupiter/DSC (P)	AA	Bette Midler		
Saturn	**RR**	**Name**	**Category I Planetary Conjunctions**	**Category II Planetary Conjunctions**
Saturn/Uranus	AA	Aretha Franklin	Mars/Jupiter	Venus/IC Pluto/PoF

Saturn	RR	Name	Category I Planetary Conjunctions	Category II Planetary Conjunctions
Saturn/Uranus	AA	Barbra Streisand		PoF/MC
Saturn/Uran (P)	AA	Bobby Murphy		Mars/PoF Sun/DSC
Saturn/Uranus	AA	Brian Wilson	Sun/Jupiter Mars/Pluto (P)	
Saturn/Uranus	AA	Martha Stewart	Neptune/NNode	
Saturn/Uranus	A	Paul McCartney	Mars/Pluto	
Saturn/Uranus	AA	Paul Simon		Uranus/MC Venus/IC (P)
Saturn/Uranus (P)	C	Rihanna	Mars/Sat/Uranus Moon/Venus	
Saturn/Uranus	AA	Ted Kaczynski	Sun/Saturn (P) Sun/Uranus (P) Mercury/Jupiter	Mercury/ASC PoF/NNode
Saturn/Uranus	AA	Vanessa Hudgens	Merc/Sat/Uranus	Moon/NNode Pluto/IC
Saturn/Uranus	A	Wayne Newton	Mars/Jupiter (P)	
Saturn/Neptune	AA	Brie Larson	Sun/Mars (P)	Uranus/MC Saturn/MC Sun/Mars(P)/ DSC
Saturn/Nept (P)	AA	Francoise Bettencourt-Meyers	Sun/Mars (P) Sun/Uranus (P) Sun/Mars/Uranus	Moon/IC
Saturn/Nept (P)	AA	Kathleen Kennedy		PoF/IC
Saturn/Neptune	AA	Patti Davis		Moon/MC NNode/ASC
Saturn/Neptune	C	Taylor Swift	Mercury/Neptune	
Saturn/Neptune	AA	Tony Blair	Moon/NNode	Mars/ASC
Saturn/Pluto	AA	Andrew Garfield		Neptune/MC Mercury/DSC NNode/IC
Saturn/Pluto (P)	C	Anne Hathaway		Sun/Jupiter (P) Sun/Venus/Jup

Saturn	RR	Name	Category I Planetary Conjunctions	Category II Planetary Conjunctions
Saturn/Pluto	AA	Carlos Santana		Saturn/Pluto/IC
Saturn/Pluto	AA	Edward Snowden	Mars/NNode (P) Jupiter/Uranus	Mercury/ASC
Saturn/Pluto (P)	AA	Jenifer (Bartoli)	Sun/Moon Sun/Venus Sun/Moon/Merc/Jupiter Sun/Jupiter	
Saturn/ASC (P)	AA	Donna Summer	Sun/Jupiter (P) Moon/Mars	Pluto/PoF (P)
Saturn/ASC (P)	AA	Evan Spiegel		Pluto/MC
Saturn/ASC (P)	AA	Jamie Lee Curtis	Sun/Venus Mercury/Saturn	
Saturn/ASC	AA	Kevin Hart	Mercury/Jupiter Saturn/NNode	
Saturn/ASC (P)	AA	Sean Connery	Sun/Neptune	
Saturn/ASC	A	Gloria Estefan		Mars/MC PoF/IC
Saturn/MC (P)	AA	Gene Wilder	Mercury/Venus Mars/Jupiter	
Saturn/MC (P)	AA	George Stephanopolous	Pluto/NNode(P) Jupiter/Saturn (P)	Mercury/PoF
Saturn/MC (P)	AA	Helmut Kohl	Sun/Mercury Sun/Uranus (Mercury/Uranus)	Venus/ASC Jupiter/PoF.
Saturn/MC	A	Justin Trudeau	Venus/NNode	
Saturn/MC	AA	Kamala Harris	Sun/Mercury Venus/Uran/Plut	NNode/ASC Saturn/MC PoF/DSC (P)
Saturn/MC/Sun/Moon	AA	Lucky Luciano	Sun/Moon (P) Sun/Mars (P) Sun/Saturn (P) Mars/Saturn Mars/Uranus	PoF/ASC Sun/Moon/ Saturn/MC Moon/MC (P)
Saturn/MC	AA	Oliver Stone	Sun/Mercury (P)	Jupiter/ASC
Saturn/MC	AA	Queen Elizabeth II	Mars/Jupiter	NNode/DSC (P)

Uranus	RR	Name	Category I Planetary Conjunctions	Category II Planetary Conjunctions
Uranus/Neptune	A	Ariana Grande	Moon/Jupiter	Uran/ASC (P) Nept/ASC (P)
Uranus/Neptune	B	Justin Bieber	Mercury/Mars Pluto/NNode	
Uranus/Pluto (P)	A	Ben Stiller		Moon/MC Jupiter/ASC
Uranus/Pluto (P)	A	Charlie Sheen	Sun/Uranus/Pluto	
Uranus/Pluto (P)	AA	Cindy Crawford	Sun/Moon Merc/Mars Mars/Saturn	
Uranus/Pluto (P)	AA	Dr. Dre	Sun/Mercury	
Uranus/Pluto	AA	Gordon Ramsay	Sun/Venus (P) Moon/Pluto Moon/Uranus (P)	
Uranus/Pluto (P)	A	Halle Berry	Moon/Mercury Mars/Jupiter	NNode/ASC Neptune/DSC Venus/IC
Uranus/Pluto	AA	J. B. Pritzker	Mercury/Venus	
Uranus/Pluto	AA	Kamala Harris	Sun/Mercury Venus/Pluto	NNode/ASC (P) (Saturn/MC)
Uranus/Pluto (P)	AA	Liz Cheney	Sun/Mercury Venus/Mars	Jupiter/IC
Uranus/Pluto	AA	Nicole Kidman		Jupiter/MC NNode/DSC
Uranus/Pluto	A	Pamela Anderson		Venus/IC
Uranus/Pluto	AA	Pierre Omidyar		Venus/ASC
Uranus/Pluto	A	Robert Downey Jr.	Mars/Uran/Pluto Sun/Venus	Pluto/PoF
Uranus/Pluto	AA	Teri Hatcher	Venus/Neptune Mars/Uranus (P) Mars/Pluto (P)	
Uranus/Pluto	AA	Trisha Yearwood	Mercury/Uranus	Jupiter/ASC

Lucky Stars, Lucky Life

Uranus	RR	Name	Category I Planetary Conjunctions	Category II Planetary Conjunctions
Uranus/ASC	A	Allison Dubois	Moon/Saturn (P) Sun/NNode	Mars/DSC Mercury/IC
Uranus/ASC	AA	Chris Evans	Jupiter/Saturn	
Uranus/ASC	AA	Conan O'Brien	Moon/Saturn	
Uranus/ASC (P)	AA	James Dean		Uran/NNode/ASC Venus/PoF
Uranus/ASC	AA	Karen Carpenter	Moon/Pluto Mercury/Jupiter	
Uranus/ASC (P)	AA	Kurt Cobain	Venus/Saturn Uranus/Pluto	Venus/DSC NNode/PoF
Uranus/MC	A	Alan Turing	Sun/Venus Sun/Pluto Venus/Pluto (P)	Jupiter/DSC
Uranus/MC	A	Andrew Yang	Moon/Mercury Mercury/Venus Neptune/NNode	Mars/PoF
Uranus/MC	AA	Brie Larson	Sun/Mars (P) Saturn/Neptune	(Saturn/MC) Sun/Mars/DSC (P)
Uranus/MC (P)	AA	Dolly Parton	Sun/Venus Mars/Saturn (P)	
Uranus/MC (P)	AA	John Carpenter		Moon/DSC
Uranus/MC (P)	AA	Judy Garland	Jupiter/NNode	Pluto/ASC
Uranus/MC	AA	Kathy Bates	Merc/Venus (P) (Mercury/Uranus)	Moon/DSC Jupiter/IC Uranus/MC
Uranus/MC (P)	AA	Michio Kaku	Sun/Mercury	Venus/IC (P)
Uranus/MC	AA	Paul Simon	Saturn/Uranus	Venus/IC
Neptune	**RR**	**Name**	**Category I Planetary Conjunctions**	**Category II Planetary Conjunctions**
Neptune/Pluto	AA	Agatha Christie		Mars/ASC Uranus/MC
Neptune/Pluto	AA	Dane Rudhyar	Mars/Nept/Pluto	
Neptune/Pluto	A	George Adamski	Neptune/NNode Pluto/NNode	Mars/IC

Neptune	RR	Name	Category I Planetary Conjunctions	Category II Planetary Conjunctions
Neptune/ASC	AA	Alice Cooper	Moon/Jupiter	
Neptune/ASC (P)	AA	Eddie Van Halen	Moon/Mercury Jupiter/Uranus	Sun/IC
Neptune/ASC	AA	Geena Davis	Jupiter/Pluto	Uranus/MC Sun/IC
Neptune/ASC	AA	William, Prince of Wales	Sun/Moon	Jupiter/MC Sun/DSC
Neptune/MC	AA	Andrew Garfield	Saturn/Pluto	Mercury/IC NNode/IC
Neptune/MC	AA	Clint Eastwood		Saturn/PoF Saturn/IC
Neptune/MC	AA	Kourtney Kardashian		Saturn/IC
Neptune/MC	AA	Matt Damon	Mercury/Pluto	
Neptune/MC	AA	Pat Boone	Venus/Uranus (P)	Mars/DSC

Pluto	RR	Name	Category I Planetary Conjunctions	Category II Planetary Conjunctions
Ascendant	A	Christopher Reeve	Sun/Mercury (P) Moon/Mars	NNode/DSC
Ascendant	AA	Eldridge Cleaver	Mars/Jupiter	NNode/DSC PoF/MC Mars/IC
Ascendant	AA	Glenn Close	Mercury/Mars	
Ascendant	AA	Judy Garland	Jupiter/NNode	Uran/MC (P)
Ascendant	AA	Merv Griffen	Sun/Pluto (P) Moon/Jupiter (P) Mercury/Venus Venus/NNode	Sun/ASC
Ascendant	AA	Michael Crichton	Venus/Mars (P)	PoF/DSC (P)
Ascendant	AA	Nancy Sinatra	Moon/Mars Venus/Mars (P)	NNode/IC
Ascendant	AA	Peter Hurkos	Mercury/NNode Mercury/Saturn Saturn/NNode	Mars/PoF

Pluto	RR	Name	Category I Planetary Conjunctions	Category II Planetary Conjunctions
Ascendant	AA	Steve Martin	Mars/Uranus Venus/NNode	Moon/IC
Ascendant	AA	Steve Perry	Venus/Jupiter	Mars/DSC
Ascendant	AA	Steven Segal	Sun/Jupiter Moon/Neptune	PoF/DSC
Ascendant	AA	Tim Robbins	Sun/NNode Mercury/Neptune Jupiter/Neptune	Mars/MC
Ascendant	AA	Will Ferrell	Moon/Neptune Uranus/Pluto	
MC	AA	Chris Evert	Sun/Mercury Moon/Venus Moon/Saturn Venus/Saturn Jupiter/Uranus	NNode/PoF
MC (P)	AA	Prince	Neptune/NNode.	Moon/IC
MC	AA	Sergio Leone		Moon/ASC Sun/PoF (Sun/IC)

Part of Fortune	RR	Name	Category I Planetary Conjunctions	Category II Planetary Conjunctions
Sun (P)	AA	Billie Jean King	Pluto/NNode	
Sun (P)	AA	Catherine Deneuve	Moon/NNode Mars/Saturn Moon/NNode (P)	
Sun	AA	Isabelle Ferarri	Merc/Jupiter (P)	Moon/ASC Venus/DSC Pluto/MC
Sun/Mercury	AA	Ron Howard	Sun/Mercury (P) Moon/NNode (P)	Nept/DSC(P) Uranus/IC
Sun	AA	Sergio Leone		Moon/ASC Pluto/MC (SUN/IC)
Sun/Nept (P)	AA	Sigourney Weaver	Sun/Neptune (P) Mars/Pluto	Moon/ASC Jupiter/MC Neptune/PoF

Part of Fortune	RR	Name	Category I Planetary Conjunctions	Category II Planetary Conjunctions
Moon (P)	AA	Andy Gibb	Sun/Mercury Jupiter/Neptune Jup/NNode (P) Nept/NNode	Pluto/DSC
Moon	AA	Bruce Lee	Venus/Mars Jupiter/Saturn	
Moon	AA	David Copperfield	Venus/Uranus	Sun/ASC
Moon	AA	Jennifer Aniston	Jupiter/Uranus	Saturn/DSC
Moon	AA	Leonard Cohen	Venus/Neptune	Sun/ASC
Moon	AA	Robert Wagner	Sun/Venus (P)	
Moon	AA	Steffi Graff	Venus/Saturn (Jupiter/Uranus)	Sun/ASC
Moon	AA	The Amazing Kreskin	Mercury/NNode	
Mercury	AA	Albert Einstein	Mercury/Saturn	Saturn/PoF
Mercury	C	Emma Roberts	Uranus/Neptune NNode/Saturn	
Mercury	AA	George Stephanopoulos	Jupiter/Saturn	Jupiter/Sat/MC Pluto/NNode
Mercury	AA	Harrison Ford	Sun/Moon	PoF/ASC
Mercury (P)	AA	Jessica Lange	Sun/Venus (P) Mars/NNode	Jup/DSC (P) Neptune/ IC
Mercury	AA	Joseph Di Mambro	Venus/Pluto (P)	
Mercury (P)	AA	Lamar Kendrick	Mercury/Mars	Jupiter/DSC Mars/PoF (P)
Mercury	AA	Ron Howard	Sun/Mercury (P) Moon/NNode (P)	Nept/DSC (P) Uranus/IC
Mercury	AA	Willie Mays	Moon/Saturn Venus/NNode (P)	
Mercury	AA	Zandaya	Venus/Mars (P)	
Venus	AA	Dick Clark	Sun/Mars(P) Mercury/Mars(P)	NNode/DSC

Part of Fortune	RR	Name	Category I Planetary Conjunctions	Category II Planetary Conjunctions
Venus	AA	Julio Iglesias	Sun/Merc/Nept Merc/Nept (P) (Jupiter/NNode)	Jupiter/MC NNode/MC
Venus (P)	AA	Liliane Bettencourt	Sun/Jupiter Mercury/Saturn	
Venus	AA	Mitt Romney	Moon/Jupiter (P)	(Moon/Jupiter/ DSC) Venus/MC
Mars	A	Andrew Yang	Moon/Mercury Mercury/Venus	Uranus/MC Neptune/ NNode
Mars (P)	AA	Barry Bonds	Venus/Mars	Mars/PoF (P)
Mars (P)	AA	Bobby Murphy	Saturn/Uranus (P)	Sun/DSC
Mars (P)	AA	H. G. Wells	Mars/Uranus Sun/NNode	Uranus/PoF
Mars	AA	Heather Locklear	Mercury/Mars Venus/Uranus Jupiter/Saturn	Sun/DSC
Mars	AA	Leonardo DiCaprio	Sun/Venus (P) Merc/Uranus (P)	
Mars	AA	Peter Hurkos	Merc/NNode (P) Mercury/Saturn Saturn/NNode	Pluto/ASC
Jupiter (P)	AA	Diane Keaton		
Jupiter (P)	AA	Dustin Hoffman	Moon/Nept (P)	
Jupiter	AA	Gwen Stefani	Mercury/Uranus	Moon/DSC Saturn/IC
Jupiter (P)	AA	Henry Kissinger	Sun/Mercury	
Jupiter	AA	Helmut Kohl	Sun/Mercury Sun/Uranus (Mercury/Uranus)	Venus/ASC
Jupiter (P)	AA	Jason Alexander	Mercury/NNode	Moon/IC
Jupiter (P)	AA	Jeffree Star	Venus/Pluto Mercury/Uranus	Mars/MC

Part of Fortune	RR	Name	Category I Planetary Conjunctions	Category II Planetary Conjunctions
Jupiter	AA	Justin Timberlake	Moon/Nept (P) Jupiter/Saturn (P)	Mars/DSC
Jupiter	AA	Olivia Newton-John	Moon/Uranus Mercury/Venus Venus/Pluto	Jupiter/IC
Jupiter/Nept (P)	AA	Mark Wahlberg	Mercury/Saturn/ Mars/NNode	
Jupiter/Pluto	AA	Maria Shriver	Merc/Nept (P) Jupiter/Pluto (P)	Uranus/IC
Saturn (P)	AA	Clint Eastwood		Neptune/MC
Saturn	AA	Dwayne Johnson	Venus/Mars	Saturn/PoF
Saturn (P)	AA	Goldie Hawn		Moon/NNode/ DSC/Jup/MC
Saturn	A	Jane Roberts	Sun/Moon Sun/NNode Moon/NNode Jupiter/NNode	PoF/Saturn
Saturn	A	Joe Montana	Moon/Uranus Jupiter/Pluto (P)	
Saturn (P)	AA	Kevin Costner	Jupiter/Uranus	
Jupiter/Uranus	AA	Drake (Graham)		Mercury/IC
(Uranus)	A	Rachel Ray	Mercury/Venus Moon/Venus (P) Moon/Pluto	Jupiter/ASC (P)
Neptune	AA	Amelia Earhart	Moon/Pluto Venus/Jupiter (P) Mars/Jupiter (P) Saturn/Uranus (P)	
Neptune	AA	Hugh Hefner		Uran/DSC (P)
Neptune (P)	AA	Jane Fonda		Pluto/DSC (P) Jupiter/ASC
Neptune (P)	AA	Jerry Lewis	Sun/Uranus (P) Venus/Jupiter (P)	Sun/Uran/MC
Neptune	AA	Kurt Russell	Sun/Jupiter	Jupiter/NNode

Lucky Stars, Lucky Life

Part of Fortune	RR	Name	Category I Planetary Conjunctions	Category II Planetary Conjunctions
Neptune (P)	AA	Mark Wahlberg	Mercury/Saturn Mars/NNode	Jupiter/Nept/ PoF
Neptune	AA	Nick Nolte	Jupiter/Saturn (P)	Jupiter/ASC (P) Saturn/ASC
Neptune	AA	Roman Polanski	Venus/Jupiter (P)	Moon/IC
Neptune	AA	Victor Borge	Mercury/Uranus	Venus/MC Pluto/NNode
Pluto	AA	Aretha Franklin	Mars/Jupiter Jupiter/Uranus	Venus/IC
Pluto (P)	AA	Donna Summer	Sun/Jupiter (P) Moon/Mars	
Pluto	AA	Herb Alpert	Moon/Saturn (P)	Jupiter/IC
Pluto (P)	AA	Janis Joplin		Saturn/IC NNode/DSC (P)
Pluto	A	Morgan Freeman		
Pluto (P)	AA	Muhamad Ali	Moon/Mercury	Venus/DSC (P)
Pluto	AA	Rami Malek	Jupiter/Saturn	Moon/IC
Pluto	A	Robert Downey Jr.	Sun/Venus Mars/Uranus Uranus/Pluto	
Pluto (P)	AA	Tiger Woods		Moon/IC
Ascendant (P)	AA	Clint Black	Sun/Moon (P) Sun/Mercury Moon/Merc (P) Mercury/Jupiter Merc/Venus (P) Venus/Jupiter (P) Mars/Saturn	(Pluto/PoF)
Ascendant	AA	Harrison Ford	Sun/Moon (NNode/Uranus)	Mercury/MC
Ascendant	A	Jane Roberts	Sun/Moon Sun/NNode Moon/NNode	Saturn/PoF

Part of Fortune	RR	Name	Category I Planetary Conjunctions	Category II Planetary Conjunctions
Ascendant	AA	Lucky Luciano	Sun/Moon (P) Sun/Saturn (P) Sun/Uranus Moon/Saturn (P) Mars/Saturn Mars/Uranus	Sun/Moon/ Saturn/MC
Ascendant	AA	Marlon Brando	Sun/Moon	Uranus/IC
Ascendant	AA	Marshall Applewhite	Sun/Moon Jupiter/Pluto	
Ascendant	AA	Martin Sheen	Sun/Moon Jupiter/Saturn(P)	Mars/DSC
Ascendant	AA	Princess Stephanie of Monaco	Sun/Moon Mercury/Venus Uranus/Pluto	Jupiter/MC
Ascendant	A	Salman Rushdie	Sun/Moon Sun/Uranus Moon/Uranus	Mercury/IC
MC	AA	Barbra Streisand	Saturn/Uranus(P)	
MC	AA	Bill Mahler	Mars/Saturn Jupiter/Pluto	
MC	AA	Joseph McCarthy		Mars/DSC NNode/Pluto
Descendant	AA	Demi Moore	Sun/Venus Mercury/Neptune	
Descendant	AA	Donald Trump	Sun/NNode/Uran Venus/Saturn	Mars/ASC
Descendant	AA	Kamala Harris	Sun/Mercury Venus/Pluto Uranus/Pluto	NNode/ASC (Saturn/MC)
Descendant (P	AA	Michael Crichton	Venus/Mars/(P)	Pluto/ASC
Descendant	AA	Steven Seagal	Sun/Jupiter	Pluto/ASC
IC	AA	Charles Manson	Sun/Venus Moon/NNode Mars/Neptune (P)	Mercury/DSC Jupiter/DSC
IC	AA	James Van Praagh	Sun/Merc/Pluto	NNode/MC

Lucky Stars, Lucky Life

Part of Fortune	RR	Name	Category I Planetary Conjunctions	Category II Planetary Conjunctions
IC	AA	Keith Richards	Mars/Uranus NNode/Pluto (P)	Moon/MC
North Node	AA	Bob Barker		Mars/ASC (P) Moon/IC Neptune/MC
North Node (P)	AA	Carol Burnett	Sun/Venus	
North Node	AA	Chris Evert	Sun/Mercury Moon/Saturn Moon/Venus Jupiter/Uranus	Pluto/MC (P)
North Node (P)	AA	Jann Werner	Mars/Saturn	Saturn/IC (P)
North Node	AA	Johnny Mathis		Sun/MC
North Node	AA	Katy Perry	Sun/Pluto (P) Moon/Saturn (P)	Mercury/ASC
North Node	AA	Kurt Cobain	Venus/Saturn Uranus/Pluto	Uranus/ASC Venus/DSC
North Node	AA	Ted Kaczynski	Sun/Uranus (P) Sun/Saturn	Merc/ASC (P)

North Node	RR	Name	Category I Planetary Conjunctions	Category II Planetary Conjunctions
Sun	A	Allison Dubois	Moon/Saturn (P)	Mars/DSC Mercury/IC
Sun (P)	AA	Bo Derek	Mercury/Saturn	Moon/IC
Sun	B	Brooke Shields	Venus/Jupiter Uranus/Pluto	
Sun	AA	Denzel Washington	Sun/Mercury Jupiter/Uran (P)	Sun/NNode/ Mercury/IC
Sun/Uranus	AA	Donald Trump	Venus/Saturn	Mars/ASC PoF/DSC
Sun (P)	AA	Guglielmo Marconi	Venus/Pluto (P)	Jupiter/DSC
Sun	AA	H. G. Wells	Mars/Uranus	Mars/PoF (P) Uranus/PoF
Sun	C	Howard Stern	Sun/Mercury Sun/Venus Mercury/Venus	NNode/Merc

North Node	RR	Name	Category I Planetary Conjunctions	Category II Planetary Conjunctions
Sun	A	Jane Roberts	Moon/NNode	Saturn/ASC Saturn/PoF
Sun	AA	Joseph Di Mambro	Venus/Pluto (P)	Mercury/PoF
Sun	A	Nayib Bukele	Jupiter/Saturn (P)	
Sun	X	Rhonda Byrne	Sun/Mercury (P) Sun/Jupiter (P) Mercury/Jupiter Mercury/NNode Jupiter/NNode	
Sun	AA	Stephen Curry	Saturn/Uranus	
Sun(P)	AA	Tim Robbins	Merc/Jup/Nept	Mars/MC Pluto/ASC
Moon	C	Arthur Miller	Mercury/Venus Mars/Neptune	
Moon	AA	Barry White	Mercury/Jupiter Venus/Mars	Moon/NNode/ DSC
Moon (P)	AA	Catherine Deneuve	Mars/Saturn Pluto/NNode	
Moon (P)	AA	Charles Manson	Sun/Venus Mars/Neptune (P)	Mercury/DSC Jupiter/DSC PoF/IC
Moon	AA	Goldie Hawn	Venus/Saturn	NNode/DSC Jupiter/MC
Moon	AA	Jack Black	Mercury/Uranus	Jupiter/IC
Moon	AA	Jamie Lee Curtis	Sun/Venus Mercury/Saturn	Saturn/ASC
Moon (P)	AA	Jim Jones	Moon/Uranus Jupiter/Pluto	
Moon	AA	Joseph Gordon-Levett	Jupiter/Saturn (P)	
Moon	A	Orlando Bloom	Mercury/Mars (P)	
Moon	C	Paris Hilton	Sun/Mercury (P) Jupiter/Saturn (P)	
Moon	AA	Robin Williams	Mars/Uranus	Merc/Pluto/ MC

Lucky Stars, Lucky Life 129

North Node	RR	Name	Category I Planetary Conjunctions	Category II Planetary Conjunctions
Moon (P)	AA	Ron Howard	Sun/Mercury (P)	Sun/Merc/PoF Uranus/IC Neptune/DSC.
Moon (P)	C	Ryan Reynolds	Sun/Moon Sun/NNode Mars/Uranus	
Moon	X	Sathya Sai Baba	Sun/Venus (P) Sun/Saturn Moon/Pluto	
Moon	AA	Tony Blair	Saturn/Nept (P)	Mars/ASC
Moon	AA	Vanessa Hudgens	Merc/Uranus (P) Mercury/Saturn Saturn/Uranus	Pluto/IC
Mercury	AA	Adam Driver	Merc/Uran/MC	
Mercury	AA	Amazing Kreskin		Moon/PoF (Jupiter/IC) (Saturn/DSC)
Mercury	C	Howard Stern	Sun/Mercury Sun/Venus Sun/NNode Mercury/Venus	Neptune/IC PoF/MC (P)
Mercury	AA	Jason Alexander		Moon/IC
Mercury	AA	Kendall Jenner	Venus/Pluto (P)	
Mercury (P)	AA	Peter Hurkos	Saturn/NNode	Mars/PoF (P) (Pluto/ASC)
Mercury	DD	Pink	Sun/Saturn Venus/Saturn	
Mercury	X	Rhonda Byrne	Sun/Mercury (P) Sun/Jupiter (P) Sun/NNode Mercury/Jupiter Jupiter/NNode	
Mercury	AA	Vincent Price	Mercury/Saturn Venus/Neptune	
Mercury	A	Zsa Zsa Gabor	Sun/Mars/Uranus	
Venus	AA	Bob Denver	Sun/Mercury	Sun/DSC
Venus	C	Courtney Cox	Moon/Pluto	

North Node	RR	Name	Category I Planetary Conjunctions	Category II Planetary Conjunctions
Venus	AA	Elvis Presley	Sun/Mercury	
Venus	AA	Imelda Marcos	Mars/Neptune (P)	Sun/ASC(P)
Venus (P)	AA	Jimmy Carter	Venus/Neptune Nept/NNode (P)	
Venus	A	Justin Trudeau		Saturn/MC
Venus	AA	Kyle Jenner		Mars/MC
Venus/Mars	AA	Merv Griffin	Sun/Pluto (P) Moon/Jupiter (P) Mercury/Venus Mars/NNode	Uranus/MC
Venus	AA	Ricky Martin	Moon/Mars	Jupiter/DSC
Venus	A	Sidney Omar	Sun/Mercury Moon/Venus (Moon/Pluto) Pluto/NNode	NNode/MC
Venus	AA	Steve Martin	Mars/Uranus	Pluto/ASC
Venus (P)	AA	Timothy McVeigh	Sun/Mercury Venus/Saturn (P) Saturn/NNode	
Venus (P)	AA	Willie Mays	Moon/Saturn	Mercury/PoF
Mars	C	Beyonce Knowles	Venus/Pluto Jupiter/Saturn	
Mars	A	Camila Cabello	Merc/Venus (P) Jupiter/Uranus	Neptune/MC
Mars	AA	Donald Glover	Venus/Mars Jupiter/Uran (P)	
Mars (P)	AA	Edward Snowden	Saturn/Pluto Jupiter/Uranus	Mercury/ASC
Mars	A	Gretchen Whitmer	Sun/Mercury Sun/Venus (P) Jupiter/Neptune	Uranus/DSC
Mars	AA	Jessica Lange	Sun/Venus (P)	Merc/PoF (P) Jupiter/DSC Neptune/IC
Mars	A	Jada Smith	Venus/Pluto Jupiter/Neptune	Moon/MC Saturn/DSC
Mars	C	Lance Armstrong	Sun/Venus/Pluto Jupiter/Neptune	

North Node	RR	Name	Category I Planetary Conjunctions	Category II Planetary Conjunctions
Mars	AA	Mark Wahlberg	Mercury/Saturn Jupiter/Neptune	Nept/PoF(P)
Mars	AA	Pele	Jupiter/Saturn (P)	
Mars	AA	Simone Biles	Sun/Mercury Sun/Venus	
Jupiter (P)	AA	Andy Gibb	Sun/Mercury (Jupiter/Neptune)	Moon/PoF (P) Pluto/DSC
Jupiter	AA	Carrie Fisher	Sun/Neptune Venus/Jupiter	
Jupiter	AA	Gloria Gaynor	Sun/Venus Mars/Uranus (P)	
Jupiter	A	Halsey	Moon/Mars Venus/Jupiter/ NNode	
Jupiter	A	James Van Praagh	Sun/Mercury (P) Sun/Merc/Pluto Venus/Neptune	
Jupiter (P)	A	Jane Roberts	Sun/Moon Sun/NNode Moon/NNode	Saturn/ASC PoF/ASC Saturn/PoF
Jupiter	AA	Judy Garland		Pluto/ASC Uranus/MC (P)
Jupiter	AA	Julio Iglesias	Sun/Merc/Nept	Venus/PoF.
Jupiter	AA	Kurt Russell	Sun/Jupiter	Neptune/PoF Uranus/ASC
Jupiter (P)	X	Rhonda Byrne	Sun/Mercury (P) Sun/Jupiter (P) Sun/NNode Mercury/Jupiter Merc/NNode (P)	
Jupiter	AA	Stedman Graham	Sun/Mercury Sun/Jup/NNode	Pluto/MC
Saturn	A	Celine Dion	Sun/Saturn Merc/Venus (P) Moon/Mars	Saturn/MC
Saturn	C	Emma Roberts	Uranus/Neptune	Mercury/PoF
Saturn (P)	AA	John Fogerty		

North Node	RR	Name	Category I Planetary Conjunctions	Category II Planetary Conjunctions
Saturn	AA	Kevin Hart	Mercury/Jupiter	Mars/MC Moon/IC
Saturn	AA	Peter Hurkos	(Mercury/Saturn) Merc/NNode (P)	Mars/PoF (P) (Pluto/ASC)
Saturn	AA	Timothy McVeigh	Sun/Mercury Venus/Saturn (P) Venus/NNode	
Uranus	X	Abraham Lincoln	(Mercury/Pluto) (Saturn/Neptune)	
Uranus	AA	Adam Driver	Merc/Uranus/MC	
Uranus	AA	Augusto Pinochet	Moon/Neptune	
Uranus	AA	Barack Obama		
Uranus	A	Bill Clinton	Venus/Nept (P)	Venus/ASC Neptune/ASC
Uranus (P)	AA	Danny Glover	Sun/Saturn (P)	
Uranus	AA	Donald Trump	Sun/Uranus Venus/Saturn	Mars/ASC PoF/DSC
Uranus	C	George Armstrong Custer	Sun/Saturn (P)	
Uranus	AA	George W. Bush	Moon/Jupiter Mercury/Pluto Mercury/Mars	Mercury/ASC
Uranus	AA	Heather Locklear	Mercury/Mars	
Uranus (P)	C	Leonard Nimoy	Merc/NNode (P) Mercury/Uranus	
Uranus (P)	AA	Linda Ronstadt	(Sun/Saturn)	
Uranus (P)	AA	Slyvester Stallone	Mercury/Pluto (P)	Jupiter/MC Moon/MC
Uranus (P)	A	William Shatner		
Neptune	A	Andrew Yang	Moon/Mercury	Mars/PoF

North Node	RR	Name	Category I Planetary Conjunctions	Category II Planetary Conjunctions
Neptune	AA	Andy Gibb	Sun/Mercury (Jupiter/Neptune) Jupiter/NNode Mercury/Venus	Moon/PoF (P) Pluto/DSC Uranus/MC
Neptune (P)	A	Ellen DeGeneres	Sun/Venus Mars/Saturn (Jupiter/Neptune)	
Neptune (P)	AA	Jimmy Carter	Venus/Neptune Venus/NNode	
Neptune	AA	Joseph Di Mambro	Venus/Pluto (P) NNode/Neptune	Mercury/PoF
Neptune	AA	Lee Iacocca		Mercury/DSC
Neptune	AA	Leonardo DiCaprio	Sun/Venus Mercury/Uranus	Mars/PoF
Neptune	AA	Martha Stewart	Saturn/Uranus	
Neptune	AA	Prince		Pluto/MC Moon/IC
Pluto	AA	Angela Davis	Mars/Uranus	
Pluto	DD	Barry Goldwater	(Sun/Uranus) Merc/Uranus (P)	
Pluto	AA	Billie Jean King	Moon/Neptune	Sun/PoF
Pluto	AA	Dennis Rodman		Jupiter/PoF Neptune/MC
Pluto	AA	Diana Ross		
Pluto (P)	A	George Adamski	Neptune/Pluto Neptune/NNode	Mars/IC (P)
Pluto	AA	George Clooney	Moon/Saturn	
Pluto	AA	George Stephanopoulos	Jupiter/Saturn	Mercury/PoF Jup/Saturn/MC
Pluto	A	Jerry Springer		Mercury/IC
Pluto	DD	Joe Frazier	Mars/Uranus (P)	Mars/Uran/PoF
Pluto	AA	John Denver	Mars/Uranus (P)	
Pluto	AA	Joseph MCCarthy		Mars/DSC PoF/MC

North Node	RR	Name	Category I Planetary Conjunctions	Category II Planetary Conjunctions
Pluto (P)	X	Julia Louise-Dryfuss	Sun/Saturn Sun/Mercury	
Pluto (P)	B	Justin Bieber	Mercury/Mars Neptune/Uranus	
Pluto (P)	A	Keith Richards	Mars/Uranus	Moon/MC PoF/IC
Pluto	AA	Marilyn Monroe	Sun/Mercury	
Pluto	A	Randy Newman		Saturn/PoF
Pluto	AA	Susan Boyle		PoF/DSC
Pluto	A	Sydney Omar	Sun/Mercury Moon/Venus (Moon/Pluto) Venus/Pluto (P)	NNode/MC Venus/NNode
Pluto	AA	Victor Borge	Mercury/Uranus	Neptune/PoF (Venus/MC)
Pluto	AA	Wayne Gretzky	Jupiter/Saturn	Sun/ASC
Ascendant (P)	AA	Arsenio Hall	Sun/Moon Jupiter/Pluto	Venus/IC
Ascendant	A	Halle Berry	Moon/Mercury Mars/Jupiter Uranus/Nept (P)	Neptune/DSC Venus/IC
Ascendant	AA	Jake Gyllenhaal	Mercury/Nept (P) Jupiter/Saturn (P)	
Ascendant	AA	James Brolin	Mercury/Pluto (P) Jupiter/Saturn	
Ascendant	AA	James Stewart	Venus/Neptune	
Ascendant	AA	Kamala Harris	Sun/Mercury Venus/Pluto Uranus/Pluto	PoF/DSC Saturn/MC
Ascendant	AA	Kevin Hart	Mercury/Jupiter	Sat/NNode/ASC Mars/MC Moon/IC
Ascendant	AA	Lisa Kudrow		Mars/IC
Ascendant	AA	Michele Ferrero	Sun/Venus (P)	Mercury/MC

North Node	RR	Name	Category I Planetary Conjunctions	Category II Planetary Conjunctions
Ascendant	AA	Patti Davis	Saturn/Neptune	Moon/MC
Ascendant	AA	Tom Brady		Mars/PoF
MC	AA	Carl Sagan	Sun/Venus Mercury/Jupiter Mars/Neptune	
MC	A	Celine Dione	Sun/Saturn Moon/Mars Merc/Venus (P)	Sun/MC Saturn/MC
MC	AA	Clara Morgane	Mercury/Mars (P) Jupiter/Saturn (P)	Moon/ASC Pluto/IC
MC (P)	AA	Claude Vorhilon (RAEL)	Sun/Neptune Mars/Jupiter	
MC (P)	AA	Donald Glover	Venus/Mars Jupiter/Uran (P)	
MC (P)	AA	James Van Praagh	Sun/Mercury (P) Sun/Merc/Pluto	PoF/IC
MC	AA	Julio Iglesias	Sun/Mercury/Neptune Merc/Nept (P) Jupiter/MC (P)	Venus/PoF
MC	AA	Mary Tyler Moore	Sun/Jupiter	
MC	AA	Robert Redford	Moon/Mercury/Nept/Moon/Merc (P)	Sun/IC
MC	AA	Rod Sterling	Sun/Jupiter Sun/Mercury	
Descendant	AA	Cameron Diaz	Sun/Mars	Venus/ASC
Descendant	AA	Dick Clark	Sun/Mars/(P) Mercury/Mars (P)	Venus/PoF
Descendant	AA	Eldridge Cleaver	Mars/Jupiter	Pluto/ASC
Descendant	AA	Goldie Hawn	Moon/NNode	Saturn/PoF(P) Jupiter/MC
Descendant	AA	Janis Joplin		Saturn/IC PoF/Pluto (P)

North Node	RR	Name	Category I Planetary Conjunctions	Category II Planetary Conjunctions
Descendant	AA	Norman Schwarzkopf	Sun/Mercury	Uranus/MC
Descendant	AA	Queen Elizabeth II	Mars/Jupiter	Saturn/MC
(IC)	AA	Adam Driver	Merc/Uranus (P)	Mercury/IC Uranus/MC
IC	AA	Adam Schiff	Sun/Venus (P)	Saturn/DSC
IC	AA	Al Pacino	Sun/Saturn (P)	
IC	AA	Andrew Garfield	Saturn/Pluto	Neptune/MC Mercury/DSC
IC	AA	Burt Bacharach		Sun/PoF.
IC (P)	AA	George Lucas		
IC	AA	Keifer Sutherland	Uranus/Pluto	Venus/ASC
IC	AA	Khloe Kardashian	Sun/Venus Mercury/Venus Mars/Saturn	Uranus/MC
IC	AA	Michelle Mone	Sun/Mercury (P) Sun/Uranus (P) Merc/Uranus (P)	Moon/IC
IC	AA	Nancy Sinatra	Mars/Uranus	Pluto/ASC

Lucky Stars, Lucky Life

BIBLIOGRAPHY

- Carter, Lance, *Planetary Patterns and High Focus Planets in Spherical Astrology*, Light Corps, 2010
- Cunningham, Donna, *The Stellium Handbook*, 2013
- De Vore, Nicholas, *Encyclopedia of Astrology*, Philosophical Library, 1947
- Jansky, Robert C., *Interpreting the Aspects, Astro Analytics*, 1978
- Jones, Marc Edmund, *The Guide to Horoscope Interpretation*, Quest Books, 1981.
- Lundsted, Betty, *Astrological Insights Into Personality*, Astro Computing Services, 1980
- Mayeda, Alan, *Ten Key Feature of Fame and Fortune - An Astrologers Look into the Celestial DNA of Celebrities*, American Federation of Astrologers, 2022
- Mitchell, Glenn, *Discover the Aspect Pattern in Your Birth Chart*, Llewellyn Publications, 2020
- Pelletier, Robert, *Planets in Aspect - Understanding Your Inner Dynamics*, Para Research, 1974
- Perry, Wendell C., *Behind the Horoscope*, Llewellyn Publications, 2020
- Rudhyar, Dane, *The First Steps in the Study of Birth-Charts*, CSA Press, 1970
- Rudhyar, Dane, *The Astrological Houses - The Spectrum of Individual Experience*, Doubleday Paperback, 1972
- Tyl, Noel, *Aspects and Houses in Analysis, Volume IV*, The Principles and Practice of Astrology, Llewellyn Publications, 1974

INDEX OF NOTABLES

NAME	PAGE
Adam Schiff	55-56
Adriana Lima	66
Adolf Hitler	74-75
Al Gore	73
Alex Trebek	62
Angela Davis	43, 77
Ann Mary Robertson Moses	7
Anthony Fauci	63-64
Archbishop Desmond Tutu	28
Art Garfunkel	45
Augusto Pinochet	26
Ayatollah Khomeini	26, 72-73
Barack Obama	73
Barbara Stanwyck	13
Barry Goldwater	26, 77
Bernard Marcus	69
Bernardo Bertolucci	62
Bill Clinton	64, 73
Bill Gates	44
Billie Jean King	77
Boris Johnson	58
Brian de Palma	62
Bruce Lee	62
Charles Manson	25
Chelsea Manning	35-36
Chris Evans	66
Christina Aguilera	66
Clara Morgane	66
Dali Lama	28
Daniel Ellsberg	35, 71-72
David Berkowitz	25
Dennis Rodman	77
Diane Keaton	82-83
Dione Warwick	62
Donald Trump	18, 26, 35-37, 64, 68, 73
Emma Stone	40
Emperor Hiroshito of Japan	58
Elizabeth Kubler-Ross	40
Faye Dunaway	62
Fidel Castro	77
General Armstrong Custer	71
George Adamski	48
George W. Bush	73
George Clooney	77
George Orwell	37
George Stephanopoulos	64-65, 77
George Wallace	66
Gina Lollobrigida	42
Gordon Ramsay	54-55
Helmut Kohl	46
Hillary Clinton	73
Howard Hughes	27
Imelda Marcos	21-22
J. R. R. Tolkien	47-48
Jair Bolsonaro	26
Jake Gyllenhaal	66
James Brolin	62
Jay Leno	22
Jerry Seinfeld	22
Jessica Alba	62, 66
Jim Jones	24-25, 74
Joan Baez	62
Joe Frazer	77
John Denver	77
John Lennon	62-63
Joseph di Mambro	73-74
Joseph Gordon-Levitt	66
Joseph McCarthy	77
Justin Bieber	47, 77
Justin Timberlake	66
Justin Trudeau	46
Kamala Harris	46
Katy Perry	4-5, 40
Keith Richards	77
Lance Armstrong	70
Linda Evans	58
Leona Helmsley	50-51
Lucky Luciano	13-14, 34-35
Mark Wahlberg	70
Mark Zuckerberg	41
Marshall Applewhite	25-26, 74
Martin Sheen	62
Martin Scorsese	52
Martin Luther	41
Mary Baker Eddy	46
Meg Ryan	42
Megan, Duchess of Sussex	66
Michele Ferrero	58-59
Miley Cyrus	47
Nicholas Sarkozy	26
Nick Jonas	47

Nick Nolte	62
Niels Bohr	38-39
Oprah Winfrey	53
Oscar Pistorius	48
Padre Pio	40
Paramahansa Yogananda	28
Paul Simon	45
Pele	62, 70
Placido Domingo	60
Pope Paul II	28
Rami Malek	66
Queen Elizabeth II	46
Randy Newman	77
Raquel Welch	62
Rhonda Byrne	11-12
Ricardo Montalban	80-81
Richard Gere	42
Richard Nixon	72
Richard Pryor	62
Rick Warren	56-57
Ringo Starr	62-63
Roger Federer	66
Ryan O'Neal	58
Sathya Sai Baba	58
Selena Gomez	47
Simon Biles	70
Slobodan Milosevic	26
Sophia Loren	42
Susan B. Anthony	46
Susan Boyle	75 – 77
Ted Kaczynski	33-35
Teilhard de Chardin	28
Victor Borge	77
Victor Orban	26
Vito Genovese	34-35
Wally Amos	58-59
Walt Disney	44
Wayne Gretsky	63-64, 77
Wernher Von Braun	69
Wolfgang Amadeus Mozart	31, 39-40

ABOUT THE AUTHOR

Alan Mayeda has an BA in political science from UC Berkeley. He first studied astrology in the early 1970s. After serving in the US Army, he resumed his education getting an MBA. Afterwards he moved to southern California entering a career in defense electronics (Uranus) from which he is retired.

Alan is a member of several astrological organizations including the American Federation of Astrologers. In addition to natal consultations, he has written numerous articles that have appeared in various publications of a number of astrological organizations, including the American Federation of Astrologers (AFA). Alan held an astrological exhibit of celebrity charts at the Senior Centers in Costa Mesa and Newport Beach, California. He is also an instructor in Qi Gong and Tai Chi. Alan has authored two previous books: "21st Century US Aquarian Presidents and World War III" and "Ten Key Features of Fame and Fortune - An Astrologers Look into the Celestial DNA of Celebrities," the last one published by AFA.

If you wish to contact the author or would like more information about this book, please write to the author in care of the American Federation of Astrologers and we will forward your request. Both the author and the publisher would appreciate hearing from you and learning how this book may have helped you. You can reach out by email at www.astrologers.com or write to:

Alan Mayeda
c/o American Federation of Astrologers
6535 S. Rural Road
Tempe, AZ 85283

www.ingramcontent.com/pod-product-compliance
Lightning Source LLC
Chambersburg PA
CBHW070938180426
43192CB00039B/2321